Published by The Junior League of Philadelphia, Inc.

Executive Committee

Chairman	Carol MacGregor
Concept Development	Anne Berry
Book Development	Kim Schuh
Marketing	Donna Mateer
Production	Diana Castillo
Business Manager	Holly Tubiash
Treasurer	Lisa Hatheway
Secretary	Linda Gilroy
Sustainer Representative	Sue Widing

Design and Art Direction	Allemann Almquist & Jones
Studio Photography	Susan Robins
Food Styling	Maria Soriano
Prop Styling	Linda Carr
Icon Illustrations	Christine Zelinsky
Printing	Wimmer Brothers Memphis, Dallas
Typesetting	Wimmer Brothers Allemann Almquist & Jones
Editorial Assistance	Mike Mallowe Senior Editor, Philadelphia Magazine Fred Clement Free-lance Writer
Wine Consultants	Suzanne Pietryk Chaddsford Winery David Hunt Kenneth Wortley

Additional Copies of *Settings* may be obtained by writing:
Settings
The Junior League of Philadelphia, Inc.
P.O. Box 492
Bryn Mawr, Pennsylvania 19010

SETTINGS

From Our Past
To Your Presentation

Published by
The Junior League of Philadelphia, Inc.

William Penn felt the magic first. The year was 1682 and for most of the civilized world, "America" was part myth, part rumor and part mysterious continent. No one in his right mind even wanted to go there, much less dreamed of beginning a new life there. William Penn, adventurer, humanitarian, visionary, was the exception.

The crown jewel of this new world was to be Penn's "greene Country Towne" called Philadelphia, so named in honor of ancient Greek beliefs of brotherhood and friendship – the very principles upon which Penn intended to establish his new city. Over 300 years later, no city more accurately reflects the high ideals and hospitality of its founding father.

In this book, we present a travelogue of Philadelphia settings. As you would take a walking tour, first take a look at Philadelphia's landmarks and cultural institutions. Read up on the area's seasonal and special events. And when you are ready, come inside for some uniquely Philadelphian food preparation ideas and table presentation suggestions to complement your personal entertaining style.

By creating more than a cookbook, we have tried to capture our esteem for the city's traditions and our respect for its history, its culture, and its beauty. This is a book for reading, not merely consulting. Curl up with it; tuck it away near your comfortable chair for that quiet moment, that lazy, reflective half-hour. Food for the body, food for the soul.

We dedicate Settings *to all our friends who share our delight in the many opportunities a good meal has to offer: from experimentation with new tastes and innovative combinations and textures; to the variety of exciting aromas, delicious sights and new sounds; to the time we especially set aside for people who are important to us. And, we want to thank the many wonderful friends — including our professional creative team — and members of the Junior League of Philadelphia who contributed an exceptional amount of time and energy toward the development of this book.*

Finally, we offer our thanks for your support, and best wishes for many years of pleasure from Settings: From Our Past to Your Presentation.

The Junior League

The Junior League of Philadelphia, Inc. was founded in 1912 as an educational and charitable non-profit organization. During its early years, the Junior League of Philadelphia (JLP) established settlement houses to improve the quality of life in the inner city neighborhoods. During both World Wars, members not only provided direct service to war sufferers, but also played a major role in training and organizing community volunteers. When women won the right to vote, the Junior League helped to train them for this new responsibility. Working with the Pennsylvania School for Social Work during the Depression, the Junior League organized an unemployment relief program.

The mission of the JLP is two-fold: first, to prepare young women for effective volunteer participation in community affairs by providing training in community need research, program development and evaluation, fundraising, and administration and skill development; secondly, to positively address the community needs through programs which are funded and staffed by its volunteers or in collaboration with other non-profit organizations. The programs are built with the confidence that they will continue autonomously once their foundations have been established.

To meet the needs of its members and the community it serves, the JLP is multi-issued. During the past decade its programs have focused on Arts and Preservation, Family Support, Education and Youth, and Community Assistance. During the past 77 years, the JLP has donated to the Philadelphia region over 3.4 million dollars, and over 5 million volunteer hours through its community programs.

The League attracts over 100 new members each year who continue in the tradition of volunteerism for the benefit of the community in which they live. Over 20 percent also serve on Boards of more than 150 other non-profit organizations.

Table of Contents

There was love as well as awe in his heart when William Penn sent a report on his new "Sylvania" back to his associates in England:

"Of all the many places I have seen in the world, I remember not one better seated; so that it seems to me to have been appointed for a Towne." That was the beginning. Penn's "holy experiment." The first Philadelphia.

Penn's Quaker ideals and infectious pursuit of excellence set the stage for Philadelphia's future. As the nation's birthplace and first seat of government, Philadelphia ushered in America's first public parks, botanical gardens, fire insurance company, theatre, public library, hospital, zoo, even the first World Exhibition in North America, and the list continues.

Going hand in hand with Philadelphia's flair for leading a young nation was its gift for hospitality. On the fashionable second stories of Society Hill district homes, Colonial Philadelphians held "at homes" (open houses) and fancy balls. Few individuals were as skilled at influencing both the course of American destiny and the tenor of Philadelphia society as Benjamin Franklin. Holding court a short walk from Independence Hall, Franklin is credited with single-handedly bringing salon society to Philadelphia and the New World. At his parties, one could expect to bump into diplomats and spies, frontiersmen and Congressmen.

The spirit of hospitality which Benjamin Franklin helped cultivate in Philadelphia is still as alive as the ideals of the nation he helped to create.

The greatest minds in the colonies met to create the Declaration of Independence, which profoundly changed the course of American history.

A revered symbol of freedom throughout America, the Liberty Bell is on display at Independence Mall.

Valley Forge National Park commemorates where the Continental Army, led by George Washington, held its 1777–78 winter encampment.

*For over 50 years
Philadelphia's commercial
center, the Merchants'
Exchange was designed by
William Strickland as a
Greek revival masterpiece.*

*Fairmount Park's
Memorial Hall is one of
two remaining structures from
the Centennial
Exposition, the first
authentically American
World's Fair.*

*This restored 18th century
Betsy Ross House
exhibits the lifestyle of the
industrious Quaker
woman credited
with creating our flag.*

*Strafford Station is
one of the seventeen train
stations along the famous
"Main Line" of the
original Pennsylvania
Railroad.*

*City Hall is at
Philadelphia's center,
dominating its
skyline with a bronze
statue of
William Penn atop
its 37 stories.*

*Independence Hall,
considered America's most
historic building,
is where the
Declaration of Independence
was signed and the
U.S. Constitution was drafted.*

Appetizers

Gift-Wrapped Brie

6 sheets phyllo dough, approximately
   12 x 14-inches
1/3 cup butter, melted
1 4½-ounce round brie
3 tablespoons Rhubarb Chutney (recipe
   follows)
Leek strip for garnish

Preheat oven to 400 degrees.

Line a small baking pan with aluminum foil. Brush foil with a thin layer
of melted butter. Lay 1 sheet of phyllo
on foil and brush with butter. Place a
second sheet of phyllo perpendicular
over the first. Brush with butter. Lay
next 2 sheets at a 45 degree angle to the
first two, brushing each layer with
butter. Repeat with final 2 phyllo
sheets. Place brie in center. Top with
chutney (it may run down the sides).
Fold up leaves of phyllo around brie
and twist on top. Brush outside of
phyllo package with remaining butter.
Bake, uncovered, for 10-15 minutes, or
until phyllo is golden brown. Let rest
for 15 minutes before serving. Tie a
bow around the twisted phyllo using a
strip of leek that has been blanched and
cooled. Cut with sharp knife. Serve
with plain crackers.

Serves 8

Rhubarb Chutney

2 pounds fresh rhubarb (4 cups), cut
   into 3/4-inch lengths
2 cups golden raisins
2 cups chopped onions
2 cups malt vinegar or apple cider
   vinegar
3 cups sugar
1 tablespoon salt
2 tablespoons ground ginger
1¼ teaspoons pepper
1 teaspoon ground cloves
1¼ teaspoons curry powder

Combine all ingredients in a large
saucepan. Bring to a boil. Reduce heat
to medium. Cook for 45 minutes,
stirring frequently, until thickened. Use
in preparing Gift-Wrapped Brie. Store
remaining chutney in refrigerator.

Yields 5-6 cups

*This chutney is also wonderful with
Macadamia Fried Brie or as an
accompaniment to Baked Cornish Hens.*

Spicy Chicken Peanut Skewers

1/4 cup chopped onions
1 clove garlic, minced
2 scallions, chopped
1 teaspoon Oriental chili paste
2 teaspoons light soy sauce
2 teaspoons grated fresh ginger
1/2 teaspoon ground cumin
1/2 teaspoon ground coriander
1/4 cup chunky peanut butter
1 cup plain yogurt
4 boneless skinless chicken breast
   halves, sliced lengthwise into strips

Combine first 10 ingredients in mixing
bowl. Add chicken strips, tossing to
combine. Cover and refrigerate several
hours or overnight.

Soak wooden skewers in water for 30
minutes. Remove chicken from
marinade, reserving marinade. Thread
chicken onto skewers in a zig-zag
fashion, using no more than 2 strips
per skewer.

Prepare charcoal grill or preheat
broiler. Place skewers in a shallow
baking pan and broil or grill over hot
coals for 2-4 minutes per side, basting
often with reserved marinade.

Place skewers in a circle on a serving
platter. Garnish with coriander leaves
and serve immediately.

Serves 8-10

Chèvre Tartlet

Crust
3 cups flour
1/2 teaspoon salt
1 cup cold unsalted butter, cut into pieces
1/3 cup ice water

Filling
12 ounces chèvre cheese
3/4 cup ricotta cheese
3/4 cup unsalted butter, room temperature
3 egg yolks
1/3 cup flour
Salt and pepper to taste

3 tablespoon fresh rosemary or
1 teaspoon dried
3 tablespoons fresh thyme or
1 teaspoon dried
2 tablespoons chopped sun-dried tomatoes

Crust: In a food processor, combine flour and salt. Add butter and process just until mixture resembles coarse meal. With machine running, add ice water in a steady stream and process just until dough forms a ball. Wrap dough in plastic wrap and refrigerate 30 minutes. Preheat oven to 400 degrees. Roll out dough on a lightly floured surface into a rectangle, approximately 12 x 15-inches. Place pastry in a 9 x 13-inch baking pan. Trim edges and freeze 5 minutes.

Line pastry with aluminum foil and weigh down with pastry weights or dried beans. Bake for 10 minutes. Remove weights and foil and allow crust to cool. Reduce oven temperature to 375 degrees.

Filling: In a food processor, combine cheeses and butter. Process until smooth. Add egg yolks one at a time, processing after each addition. Add flour, salt and pepper to taste. Process until blended. Fill tart shell with cheese filling. Combine herbs and sun-dried tomatoes and sprinkle on tart. Bake 25-30 minutes at 375 degrees until browned and slightly puffed. Cool slightly. Cut into squares and serve.

Variation: Roll pastry 1/8-inch thick. Line 24 tartlet pans with pastry. Press another pan, which has been buttered on the outside, into first pan. Bake 7-8 minutes at 400 degrees. Remove top pan. Return to oven and bake until lightly browned. Sprinkle herbs and tomatoes over crust. Fill with cheese mixture. Bake 10-12 minutes at 375 degrees. Cool slightly and remove from pans.

Yields 20 squares

Individual tartlets with a rich chèvre cheese filling. Try preparing this recipe in a 9-inch tartlet pan and serve in wedges for an elegant brunch.

Smoked Oyster Roll

2 8-ounce packages cream cheese, softened
1 shallot, chopped
3 tablespoons mayonnaise
2 teaspoons Worcestershire sauce
1 small clove garlic, minced
1/4 teaspoon salt
Pinch pepper
Dash hot pepper sauce

2 tins smoked oysters, drained and coarsely chopped
1/2 cup chopped pistachio nuts
1/4 cup chopped parsley

In a medium mixer bowl, combine cream cheese and shallots. Blend until smooth. Add mayonnaise, Worcestershire sauce, garlic, salt, pepper and hot pepper sauce. Mix well. Roll out between 2 sheets of waxed paper until 1/4-inch thick. Form into a rectangle. Remove top sheet of waxed paper.

Arrange oysters evenly on cheese rectangle. Roll up, jelly roll fashion, using bottom of waxed paper as a guide. Combine nuts and parsley. Coat roll with nut mixture. Wrap in foil and chill.

To serve, garnish roll with parsley and serve with crackers.

Serves 10-12

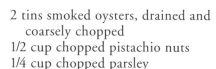

Teriyaki Shrimp with Hot Plum Sauce

24 large uncooked shrimp, peeled and
    deveined
1/3 cup oil
1/4 cup soy sauce
1/4 cup lemon juice
2 tablespoons dry sherry
2 cloves garlic, minced
1/2 teaspoon freshly ground pepper
12 slices bacon, cut in half crosswise

Hot Plum Sauce
1 cup plum preserves
2 tablespoons lemon juice
1 tablespoon ketchup
2 tablespoons brown sugar
1 tablespoon Dijon mustard

Place shrimp in a large bowl. Combine
oil, soy sauce, lemon juice, sherry,
garlic and pepper. Pour over shrimp.
Stir to combine. Cover and chill,
stirring occasionally, for several hours.

Hot Plum Sauce: Combine all
ingredients in a small saucepan and
simmer for 10 minutes. Cool.

Preheat oven to 450 degrees. In a
frying pan, cook bacon until most of
the fat is rendered, but bacon is still
pliable. Drain and set aside. Remove
shrimp from marinade. Wrap one
bacon slice around each shrimp,
securing with a toothpick. Place shrimp
on foil-lined baking dish. Bake 6
minutes. Serve with hot plum sauce.

Variation: Scallops may be substituted
for shrimp.

Yields 24 pieces

Boule of Hot Cheese

1 large boule sourdough bread
2 3-ounce packages cream cheese,
    softened
1 16-ounce container sour cream
2 cups grated Cheddar cheese
1 medium onion, chopped
4-5 fresh jalapeño peppers, seeded and
    chopped (not pickled)
1½ teaspoons Worcestershire sauce

Preheat oven to 350 degrees.

Cut off top of bread and hollow out
boule, saving top and insides of bread.
Cut insides into bite-size pieces.

Cream together cream cheese and sour
cream until blended. Add Cheddar
cheese, onion, peppers and
Worcestershire sauce. Mix thoroughly.
Fill hollowed boule with cheese
mixture. Replace top of bread. Wrap
boule in 2 or 3 sheets of aluminum foil.
Bake for 1 hour and 15 minutes.

Place boule on a serving plate.
Surround with cut up sourdough bread
and pita crisps.

Serves 12-14

Mostly Mushrooms

2 tablespoons butter
1/2 pound fresh mushrooms, chopped
1 8-ounce package cream cheese,
    softened
1/4 cup mayonnaise
1 tablespoon Worcestershire sauce
1/8 teaspoon garlic powder
Salt and freshly ground pepper to taste

Sauté mushrooms in butter until most
of the liquid has evaporated. Drain.
Combine mushrooms with cream
cheese, mayonnaise, Worcestershire
sauce, garlic powder, salt and pepper,
mixing thoroughly.

Place in a decorative bowl and
surround with an assortment of
crackers.

Yields 1½ cups

Asparagus Custard with Red Pepper Sauce

Asparagus Custard
24 medium asparagus spears
3/4 cup heavy cream
3 eggs, separated
4-6 drops hot pepper sauce
3/4 teaspoon salt
Pepper to taste

Red Pepper Sauce
2 tablespoons olive oil
1¼ cups chopped red pepper
2 tablespoons chopped onion
2 tablespoons dry vermouth
2 egg yolks
2 tablespoons lemon juice
1/2 cup butter, cut into pieces
1/4 teaspoon hot pepper sauce
1/4 teaspoon cayenne pepper
4-5 drops red food coloring (optional)

Preheat oven to 325 degrees.

Custard: Cut asparagus tips 3 inches from top, steam until tender and slice lengthwise; set aside. Trim asparagus bottoms and slice thinly. Place in saucepan with enough heavy cream to cover. Bring to a boil, lower heat and simmer 5 minutes until tender. Purée in small batches in a blender until smooth. When all is puréed, return to blender. At low speed, add egg yolks. Blend 1 minute. With blender running, add egg whites, one at a time, mixing well after each addition. Blend 1 minute. Season with hot pepper sauce, salt and pepper.

Pour mixture into 4 buttered 6-ounce custard cups. Cover each with waxed paper. Place cups in roasting pan on lower shelf of oven. Pour hot water into the roasting pan to reach 3/4 up the sides of cups. Bake 30-35 minutes, or until knife inserted in center comes out clean.

Sauce: In skillet, heat olive oil. Sauté pepper and onion 3-5 minutes. Add vermouth. Simmer 2 minutes (or place onion, pepper and vermouth in microwave container, cover and cook on high for 3-5 minutes, until tender). Transfer mixture to blender and blend until mixture is a frothy purée. In top of double boiler, whisk egg yolks with lemon juice until pale and bubbly. Set over simmering water. Whisking constantly, add butter 3-4 pieces at a time. Continue cooking, whisking constantly, until mixture thickens to consistency of pudding. Remove from heat. Set in a bowl of cool water and continue whisking until pan is cool to the touch. Whisk in hot pepper sauce, cayenne and puréed pepper mixture. If sauce is too pale, add a few drops of red food coloring.

To Serve: Invert custards onto 4 serving plates. Spoon sauce around custards and place reserved asparagus tips on top of sauce.

Serves 4

Macadamia Fried Brie

1 cup macadamia nuts, ground
3/4 cup dry bread crumbs
1 8-ounce round brie
1/2 cup flour
2 eggs, beaten
Safflower oil

Preheat oven to 350 degrees.

Mix nuts and bread crumbs. Place in a shallow bowl. Cut brie into 8 wedges. Dip brie wedges in flour, then beaten egg, then crumb mixture. Let rest on waxed paper for a few minutes. Repeat with egg and crumbs, coating completely. Heat oil to 350 degrees in a deep pan. Fry cheese, 1 or 2 pieces at a time, for 2 minutes, turning once. Drain on paper towels (can be cooled and chilled at this point). Bake fried wedges for 3-4 minutes in 350 degree oven. Serve with Rhubarb Chutney and crackers.

Serves 8

Lamb and Scallion Quesadillas

1/2 pound ground lamb
1/4 cup chopped green onions
2/3 cup shredded Monterey Jack cheese
2/3 cup shredded mozzarella cheese
2/3 cup shredded Asiago cheese
4 flour tortillas
Butter
Sour cream
Salsa (recipe follows)
8 sprigs fresh cilantro

Sauté lamb over medium heat until no longer pink. Drain. Add chopped green onions. Combine cheeses in a bowl and set aside. Melt 2 teaspoons butter in small frying pan. Place 1 tortilla in pan. Place 3 tablespoons lamb mixture on 1/2 of the tortilla. Top with 1/2 cup of the cheese mixture. Fold tortilla in half, covering filling. Cook over medium heat for 3 minutes. Turn carefully and continue cooking 3 minutes longer, until tortilla is lightly browned and cheese is melted. Repeat with remaining tortillas. Cut each tortilla into 4 wedges.

Place 2 wedges on each plate and serve with Salsa and a dollop of sour cream. Garnish with a sprig of cilantro.

Serves 8

Contributed by Under the Blue Moon

A favorite appetizer from this popular Chestnut Hill restaurant. The chef has been known to make the quesadillas with other meats, vegetables or even seafood.

Salsa

1 cup chopped and drained tomatoes, preferably fresh
1/2 cup chopped onion
1/2 cup chopped green onion
1/2 cup chopped red pepper
1/2 cup chopped green pepper
2 tablespoons cilantro, minced
1 teaspoon minced garlic
2 tablespoons olive oil
3 tablespoons red wine vinegar
Splash balsamic vinegar
1 jalapeño or hot chili pepper, seeded and minced

Combine all ingredients in bowl and refrigerate for several hours to let flavors mellow. Serve with Quesadillas or as a dip with nachos or other chips.

Yields 3 cups

Contributed by Under the Blue Moon

Sour cream is a cooling contrast to the fiery salsa.

Broiled Oysters with Bacon, Parmesan and Horseradish

30 fresh oysters
6-7 slices bacon
Lemon juice
Horseradish
Hot pepper sauce
Grated Parmesan cheese

Preheat broiler.

Open oysters. Discard top shells and loosen oyster in bottom shell. Arrange on a broiler tray. Cut bacon slices into 1½-inch long pieces and blanch for 1½ minutes. Drain and set aside.

Top each oyster with a generous squeeze of lemon juice, 1/8 teaspoon horseradish, 2-3 drops hot pepper sauce and 1 piece of blanched bacon. Sprinkle with Parmesan cheese. Broil until golden brown. Serve immediately.

Yields 30 hors d'oeuvres or serves 6-8 as a first course.

Contributed by Rollers Restaurant

Pâté du Campagne

1 pound pork fat
1 pound boneless veal
1 pound boneless pork
1 pound ham
1/2 pound chicken livers
8 cloves garlic, peeled
1/3 cup heavy cream
3 eggs
1/3 cup cognac
1 teaspoon salt
2 teaspoons white pepper
1 teaspoon allspice
1/2 teaspoon ground cinnamon
1 teaspoon ground thyme
1/2 cup flour

Preheat oven to 400 degrees.

Thinly slice 1/2 pound of the pork fat; set aside. Finely grind remaining pork fat with veal, pork and ham. Line one 3-quart or two 1½-quart molds with reserved pork fat, letting long ends hang over edge of pan.

In a blender or food processor, purée the livers, garlic, cream, eggs and cognac. Add 1/3 of the meat mixture to the processor and mix. Place the remaining meat mixture in a large mixing bowl. Add seasonings and flour. Add the processor mixture and mix thoroughly. Pour into prepared mold(s), covering top with the pork fat. Cover tightly with double thickness of aluminum foil.

Place mold(s) in a large baking pan. Fill pan with boiling water halfway up the sides of mold(s). Bake for 1½ hours for small molds or 3 hours for a large mold. Remove foil and continue baking until top is brown, about 20 minutes. After removing from oven, leave mold(s) in pan. Place weight on top of pâté until completely cooled. Cover and refrigerate until serving. Unmold onto serving plate. Serve with crackers, French or black bread and a variety of mustards.

Serves 10-12

The thin layer of pork fat which wraps the pâté bastes it and gives it extra moisture while it bakes. Excellent fare for a picnic yet elegant enough for a first course.

Crabmeat in Limes

3 large limes
3/4 cup safflower oil, divided
2 cloves garlic, minced
1 teaspoon grated fresh ginger
1/2 cup lime juice
1/3 cup dry white wine
1/3 cup chopped chives
1 teaspoon salt
3/4 teaspoon pepper
1 pound fresh crabmeat
1/2 cup grated carrot

Cut limes in half lengthwise and remove pulp. Squeeze juice from pulp to measure 1/2 cup. Set aside.

In a large skillet, heat 2 tablespoons oil. Add garlic and ginger. Sauté until golden. Add remaining oil, lime juice, wine, chives, salt and pepper. Stir to combine. Add crabmeat and cook, stirring frequently, for 5 minutes.

Spoon crabmeat mixture into 6 lime shells and garnish with grated carrot. Serve immediately.

Variation: May substitute cooked lobster, shrimp or monkfish for crabmeat.

Serves 6

Double Dip Artichoke

2 whole artichokes

Cut sharp points off leaves. Cut stems one inch from bottom of artichokes. Soak in a sinkful of cold water for 15 minutes to clean them. Place the artichokes upright in a pan with about 4 inches of water, some lemon slices and a drop of olive oil. Cook over medium heat, partially covered, until the leaves pull off easily, 30-45 minutes. Serve with dips below.

Beyond Guacamole
1 avocado
1/4 cup sour cream
1 tablespoon chopped shallots
1 teaspoon fresh lemon juice
Cayenne pepper
Salt

In a medium bowl, mash the avocado. Stir in sour cream, chopped shallots and lemon juice. Season to taste.

Sweet Red Bell Pepper Dip
1 large red bell pepper, sliced
1/4 cup pine nuts
1 teaspoon fresh sorrel
1 large clove garlic
1/4 cup sour cream
Chili powder
Salt

In food processor, chop together pine nuts, sorrel and garlic. Add pepper and process for 1-2 seconds. Blend in sour cream. Season to taste.

Serves 4

Lobster Ravioli

2 1½-pound lobsters
40 won ton wrappers
1/3 cup peeled, seeded and diced tomato
1/3 cup crème fraîche
20 fresh basil leaves
1 large egg yolk
2 tablespoons water
1 cup crème fraîche, warmed

Lobster Bisque
Shells and carcasses from lobsters
2 tablespoons olive oil
1 carrot, peeled and chopped
1 onion, peeled and chopped
1 cup water
1½ cups white wine
2 tablespoons tomato paste
1/2 cup crème fraîche
2 tablespoons butter

Boil lobsters in a large pot of boiling, lightly salted water for 7 minutes. Remove and set aside to cool. (Can be done 1 day ahead and refrigerated.) When cool, separate carcass. Remove lobster tail meat. Save claw meat for garnish. Save carcass for bisque. Lay out 20 won ton wrappers on a flat surface. Slice tail meat into 20 small pieces. Mix tomato and crème fraîche. Place lobster meat on won ton wrappers. Add approximately 1 teaspoon tomato mixture on top of lobster. Top with 1 basil leaf per wrapper. Mix egg yolk with water. Brush edges of won ton wrappers with egg mixture. Top each with remaining 20 won ton wrappers. Roll edges with pasta wheel to seal edges. Cover until ready to use.

Bisque. Chop carcasses into small pieces. Heat olive oil in a large heavy saucepan. Add carcasses and sauté for a few minutes. Add carrot and onion; cook until onion is golden. Add water, wine and tomato paste. Bring to a boil, then simmer for 20-25 minutes. Remove from heat. Strain through fine sieve set over a saucepan. Return bisque to heat and cook until reduced to approximately 1¼ cups. Lower heat. Whisk in the 1/2 cup crème fraîche. Set aside.

Bring large pot of water to a light boil. Lightly salt water. When it returns to a boil, add ravioli and cook 3-4 minutes. Remove ravioli; drain. Lower heat and simmer lobster claws until tender. Remove and cool. Gently mix ravioli with the 1 cup warmed crème fraîche, being careful not to tear the skins. Heat bisque. Adjust seasonings. Whisk in the 2 tablespoons butter.

To Serve: Place 3-4 ravioli on each of 6 plates. Drizzle lobster bisque over ravioli. Garnish with claw meat and basil sprig.

Serves 6

An elegant first course for a special dinner party. Tender lobster ravioli tossed with crème fraîche and finished with a lobster bisque is a heavenly combination, well worth the effort.

Baked Stuffed Clams

2 dozen fresh cherrystone clams (2 to 3-inch shells), well scrubbed or 2 cans chopped clams, drained
1/2 cup butter
1 medium onion, chopped
2 cloves garlic, minced
1/2 red bell pepper, chopped
1 tablespoon chopped fresh parsley
5 drops hot pepper sauce
1 tablespoon lemon juice
2/3 cup Italian bread crumbs
1 cup shredded Cheddar or Tilsit cheese

Preheat oven to 400 degrees. In a large, heavy pot, steam the clams in batches of 6 until they just open. Remove clams from shell. Place all clams in food processor fitted with a steel blade. Pulse 4-5 times to chop. Drain clams in colander. Cut any pieces that seem too large. There should be approximately 2 cups. Break apart clam shells and save 18 halves. Wash and dry reserved shells.

In a large skillet, melt butter and gently sauté onion, garlic, pepper, parsley and hot pepper sauce for 15 minutes, until onion and pepper are tender. Add drained clams, lemon juice and bread crumbs to skillet. Remove from heat. Toss to combine.

Set cleaned clam shells on sheet of foil in large baking pan. Spoon clam mixture into shells. Top with shredded cheese. Bake for 15 minutes, until cheese starts to brown. If using canned clams, spread mixture in a 9-inch quiche or pie plate and cover with cheese. Bake as above. Garnish with lemon wedges and parsley and serve with firm crackers.

Serves 6 as a first course

The variation in preparation allows the hostess the flexibility of offering it as a first course at a dinner for 6 or as an appetizer for a party of 12.

Chinese Dumplings

1 package won ton wrappers

Filling
1/2 pound ground pork
1/4 pound shrimp, peeled, deveined and minced
2 water chestnuts, finely chopped
1½ scallions, chopped
1 egg yolk, lightly beaten
3/4 teaspoon white wine
1/4 teaspoon garlic powder

Dipping Sauce
4 tablespoons soy sauce
4 tablespoons rice wine vinegar
2 teaspoons chopped green onion

Bring wrappers to room temperature. Combine ingredients for filling in a bowl and let rest for 30 minutes. Lay out 1 won ton wrapper. Place 1/2 to 1 tablespoon filling on wrapper. Fold ends toward middle and pinch closed at top. Set aside on waxed paper. Continue until all filling has been used.

Combine ingredients for dipping sauce and heat to boiling. Cool.

Heat a few inches of water in a wok or large frying pan. Place dumplings in one layer of Chinese steamer. Place covered steamer in wok and steam for 4-5 minutes or until cooked through.

Serve dumplings with cooled dipping sauce.

Serves 6-8

Salmon and Spinach Pâté with
Tomato Basil Sauce

Pâté
1½ pounds salmon fillet, cut into small
     pieces
2 egg whites
1/2 teaspoon salt
1/4 teaspoon pepper
1 tablespoon lemon juice
2 cups heavy cream

2 tablespoons butter
2 cups sliced leeks
1 10-ounce package frozen chopped
     spinach, thawed and drained
2 eggs
1/2 teaspoon salt
1/8 teaspoon pepper
1/8 teaspoon nutmeg
1/4 cup heavy cream

Tomato Basil Sauce
1 cup mayonnaise (preferably
     homemade)
1/2 cup sour cream
1 tablespoon tomato paste
2 teaspoons lemon juice
1 ripe tomato, peeled, seeded and
     chopped
1/4 cup chopped fresh basil

Preheat oven to 350 degrees.

Pâté: For salmon layers, place salmon
in bowl of food processor. Process for 1
minute. Add egg whites, salt, pepper
and lemon juice. Mix well. Place
mixture in separate bowl and stir in
cream.

For spinach layer, melt butter in skillet.
Add leeks. Sauté until softened. Place
spinach in bowl of food processor.
Process 1 minute. Add leeks, eggs, salt,
pepper and nutmeg. Mix well. Place
mixture in separate bowl and stir in
cream.

Place 1/2 of the salmon mixture in a
9 x 5-inch glass loaf pan. Make a slight
indentation lengthwise down center,
leaving salmon mixture higher around
edge of pan. Fill indentation with all
of the spinach mixture. Place remaining
salmon mixture over spinach layer and
smooth top. Cover with waxed paper.
Wrap pan in foil and place in larger
pan. Fill larger pan halfway up with
warm water. Bake for 1 hour. Let pâté
cool, then refrigerate.

Sauce: Combine all ingredients in a
bowl and refrigerate.

To Serve: Slice pâté into 1/4 to 1/2-inch
slices. Garnish with basil leaves and
serve with sauce.

Serves 14-16

*A contrast in colors, this pâté offers a
delicate combination of mousses
complemented by the tart taste of tomato
and basil.*

Cheddar and Artichokes in
Phyllo

1 17-ounce can artichoke hearts, rinsed
     and drained completely
1/2 cup sour cream
1 cup grated Cheddar cheese
2 large cloves garlic, minced
1 teaspoon oregano, crumbled
15 sheets phyllo dough, stacked
     between 2 sheets of waxed paper and
     covered with a damp cloth
1/2 cup butter, melted

Preheat oven to 375 degrees.

Squeeze artichokes to remove excess
liquid. Shred. Combine with sour
cream, Cheddar cheese, garlic and
oregano.

On a work surface, place 1 sheet
phyllo dough and brush lightly with
melted butter. Place second sheet on
top of first, brushing lightly with
butter. Repeat with 3 more sheets
(total of 5 sheets). Spread 1/3 of the
artichoke mixture in a strip along one
side of buttered phyllo stack, leaving
1-inch border of phyllo. Roll up
phyllo, beginning at filled edge, tucking in sides as you go. Place seam side
down on a buttered baking sheet.
Brush roll with melted butter. Repeat
to make 2 more rolls. Bake 25-30 minutes or until golden. Cool and cut into
bite-size pieces with serrated knife.

Yields 30 pieces

Soups

Jambalaya

1¼ to 1½ pounds smoked pork butt
1 onion, sliced
1 cup celery leaves
2 to 3 parsley sprigs
1/4 teaspoon ground red pepper
5 cups water
1/4 teaspoon black pepper
1 cup chopped celery
1/2 cup chopped onion
1 small clove garlic, minced
2 tablespoons butter
1 8-ounce can tomato sauce
1/4 cup ketchup
1/2 cup long grain rice
1 10-ounce package frozen cut okra
1 4½-ounce can shrimp
Leftover cooked chicken or turkey,
    shredded

In a large heavy saucepan, combine pork butt, onion slices, celery leaves, parsley sprigs, red pepper, water and black pepper. Bring to boiling; reduce heat, cover, simmer 30-45 minutes. Remove bone. Cut off meat and shred. Discard bone. Strain broth.

In a small saucepan, sauté celery, onion and garlic in butter until tender. Stir into broth. Add pork, tomato sauce, ketchup and uncooked rice. Bring to a boil; reduce heat. Simmer for 15 minutes. Add okra, drained shrimp and chicken or turkey. Return to boiling; reduce heat. Cover and simmer 5 minutes.

Best when served the next day.

Serves 6

Curried Shrimp Chowder

4 tablespoons butter
1 Granny Smith apple, finely chopped
1 cup finely chopped celery
2 cups finely chopped onions
2 cups water
1 pint light cream
2 tablespoons curry powder
1½ teaspoons salt
1/2 teaspoon finely ground pepper
2 to 2½ cups chicken broth, heated
1 pound cooked and peeled shrimp,
    each cut in half
1 pound white potatoes, peeled and
    diced
1 cup fresh corn

In a large saucepan, sauté the apple, celery and onions in butter until lightly browned. Add the water and simmer until almost all of the water has evaporated. Purée the mixture in a food processor until smooth. Return mixture to the saucepan; add cream, curry powder, salt and pepper and simmer over very low heat until reduced and thickened. Stir in the chicken broth. Add the shrimp and corn and simmer for a few minutes.

Meanwhile, boil diced potatoes in lightly salted water for 5 minutes; drain and add to soup mixture. Simmer soup for an additional 2 to 3 minutes. Serve immediately.

Serves 6

A hearty soup that can make a family supper when served with warm Soft Pretzels and a crock of mustard.

Mushroom Crab Bisque

6 tablespoons butter
2 cups fresh mushrooms, chopped
1 small onion, chopped
2 cloves garlic, minced
6 tablespoons flour
4 cups chicken broth
1 pound jumbo lump crabmeat
4 cups light cream
2 teaspoons Worcestershire sauce
1/2 teaspoon salt
1/2 teaspoon pepper
1/2 teaspoon celery salt
1/2 teaspoon nutmeg
1/2 cup white wine

In a 6-quart saucepan, sauté mushrooms, onion and garlic in butter for 5 minutes. Blend in flour and add broth, stirring over medium heat until smooth, about 10 minutes. Flake crabmeat and remove cartilage. Add crabmeat and remaining ingredients and bring to a light boil. Reduce heat and simmer for 10 minutes.

Serves 8-10

Both rich and creamy, this bisque of garden fresh mushrooms and the sea's finest crabmeat needs little more than a loaf of crusty French Bread to become a meal.

Shrimp and Scallop Chowder

4 medium potatoes, peeled and diced
2 medium carrots, chopped
2 stalks celery, chopped
1 large onion, chopped
4 cups chicken broth
1/4 teaspoon pepper
2 small bay leaves
1/2 teaspoon thyme
3/4 pound fresh mushrooms, sliced
2 tablespoons butter
1 pound fresh bay scallops
1/2 pound small shrimp, peeled and
   deveined
1/2 cup dry white wine
1 cup heavy cream
1 egg yolk
Salt to taste
Parsley for garnish

In large soup pot, combine potatoes,
carrots, celery and onion. Add broth
and bring to a boil. Add pepper, bay
leaves and thyme and simmer, covered,
until vegetables are tender, about 30
minutes. Remove bay leaves. In food
processor, purée until smooth. Put
purée back in soup pot.

Sauté mushrooms in butter. Add
scallops, shrimp and wine and cook
until shrimp are pink, about 2 minutes.
Stir in cream mixed with egg yolk.
Pour seafood mixture into soup pot
with vegetable mixture. Heat until
warm, being careful not to boil. Salt to
taste and garnish with parsley.

Serves 6

Hearty Chicken Soup

5 cups water
1 teaspoon salt
4 slices bacon, chopped
1 2 to 3-pound chicken
2 medium carrots, peeled and sliced
1 onion, peeled and chopped
1 package frozen mixed corn and lima
   beans
1/8 teaspoon cayenne pepper
Few sprigs fresh parsley, chopped
2 ribs celery, chopped
2 potatoes, peeled and cubed
1 10-ounce can tomatoes
1 teaspoon sugar
1 cup heavy cream
Salt and pepper to taste

Bring water and salt to a boil. Add
bacon, chicken, carrots, onion, lima
beans and corn. Add cayenne pepper,
parsley and celery. Cover and bring to a
boil, skim if necessary. Reduce heat,
cover and cook slowly for about 2
hours. Check the chicken after 1 to
1½ hours. When the chicken is tender,
remove it from the pot and cut the
meat into pieces. Discard bones and
skin. Return the chicken pieces to the
pot and continue cooking, stirring
occasionally. After the first 2 hours,
add potatoes, tomatoes and sugar.
Continue cooking for 1 more hour.
Add heavy cream. Bring mixture just to
a boil. Add salt and pepper to taste.
Serve in large soup bowls.

Serves 8

Sausage Ravioli Soup

1 pound Italian sausage, taken out of
   casing
1 cup chopped onions
2 cloves garlic, chopped
5 cups beef broth
1/2 cup water
1/2 cup dry red wine
2 cups peeled, seeded, chopped
   tomatoes
1 cup thinly sliced carrots
1/2 teaspoon basil
1/2 teaspoon fennel
1/2 teaspoon oregano
1 8-ounce can tomato sauce
1½ cups sliced fresh zucchini
3 tablespoons chopped fresh parsley
1 medium green pepper, cut into
   1/2-inch pieces
8 ounces small fresh cheese-filled
   ravioli
Freshly grated Parmesan cheese

In a large saucepan, brown sausage
and drain, reserving 1 tablespoon
of the drippings in the pan. Sauté
the onions and garlic in the drippings
until onion is tender. Add broth,
water, wine, tomatoes, carrots, seasonings, tomato sauce and sausage. Simmer uncovered for 30 minutes. Skim
fat. Stir in zucchini, parsley, green
pepper and ravioli. Cover and simmer
until vegetables are tender and ravioli
are cooked through, about 35 minutes.
Garnish with Parmesan cheese.

Serves 8

Wild Mushroom Soup

5 tablespoons butter
1 small onion, minced
2 large shallots, minced
3/4 pound fresh wild mushrooms, finely
   chopped
3 tablespoons flour
1 10½-ounce can beef consommé
1 13¾-ounce can beef broth
3 bay leaves
Salt and pepper to taste
1/2 cup heavy cream
Parsley for garnish

Melt the butter in a heavy saucepan
and add the onion and shallots. Stir in
the mushrooms and cook until quite
soft. Sprinkle in the flour, stirring
constantly. Pour in consommé and
broth; add bay leaves. Season to taste
with salt and pepper. Add cream just
before serving. Garnish with parsley.

Serves 6-8

*A rich and creamy broth offers a perfect
balance to the texture and taste of the
wild mushrooms. A surprise opener for a
dinner of intrigue.*

Creamy Cabbage and
Cheese Soup

2 tablespoons butter
1 cup chopped onion
2 cups hot water
3-4 teaspoons instant chicken bouillon
1 cup sliced carrots
1 cup pared, diced potatoes
2 cups shredded cabbage
4 tablespoons butter
1/4 cup flour
1/4 teaspoon paprika
1/4 teaspoon pepper
3 cups milk
1¼ to 1½ cups shredded Cheddar
   cheese
1 10-ounce package baby lima beans

In a large saucepan, sauté onion in
butter for 5 minutes over low heat.
Dissolve bouillon in hot water; add to
onions and bring to a boil; cover and
reduce heat to low. Add carrots,
potatoes and cabbage and cook until
vegetables are tender, about 30
minutes. Remove from heat and set
aside.

Melt remaining butter in a large Dutch
oven; blend in flour, paprika and
pepper. Allow this mixture to bubble
2-3 minutes. Remove from heat and
slowly add milk, whisking constantly.
Return to heat and cook 2-3 minutes,
continuing to whisk until thickened.
Add cheese and melt. Remove from
heat; add vegetable mixture and lima
beans. Cook over low heat until lima
beans are tender. Serve warm.

Serves 6-8

Black Bean Soup

2 cups black beans
8 cups cold water
1 clove garlic, minced
3 medium onions, chopped
1/2 cup chopped celery
4 tablespoons butter
2 bay leaves
2 tablespoons fresh parsley
1/2 teaspoon salt
1 teaspoon ground black pepper
1 meaty ham bone
Sour cream for garnish
Fresh chopped scallions for garnish
Grated Cheddar cheese for garnish

Soak beans overnight in just enough
water to cover them. Drain thoroughly.
Place beans in a large soup kettle and
fill with 8 cups of cold water. Cook
over low heat, uncovered, for 1½
hours. Sauté garlic, onion and celery in
butter. Add to soup kettle along with
bay leaves, parsley, salt, pepper and
ham bone. Cook, covered, over low
heat for 3 hours (If soup is too thick,
add water. If too thin, remove cover
and boil for 1/2 hour). Remove ham
bone from kettle; cut off meat and
return to the soup. Heat until just hot.
Serve soup topped with sour cream,
chopped scallions and grated Cheddar
cheese.

Serves 4-6

Cheese Soup in Acorn Shells

4 large acorn squash with stems and flat
  bottoms
4 cups chicken broth
1¼ cups heavy cream
Salt, pepper and nutmeg to taste
1/4 pound Gruyère cheese

Cut around stem ends of squash to
form lids; scrape out seeds and discard.
Scoop out pulp, leaving 1/2-inch thick
shell. In a medium saucepan, combine
pulp and broth and bring to a boil.
Reduce heat and simmer briskly until
liquid reduces to 2 cups, about 30
minutes. Transfer to blender or food
processor and purée until smooth. Add
cream and season with salt, pepper and
nutmeg.

Position rack in lower third of oven
and preheat oven to 400 degrees.
Divide half the cheese among the
squashes; then ladle some of the soup
over the cheese. Top with remaining
cheese. Cover with lids. Arrange squash
in shallow roasting pan. Bake until
squash is dark and tender, about 45
minutes. Place individual squash in
soup bowls and serve.

Serves 4

Cream of Senegalese

1/2 cup butter
1 head Boston lettuce, finely chopped
1 medium onion, thinly sliced
1/2 cup finely chopped fresh parsley
2 teaspoons fresh curry powder
3 tablespoons flour
1 teaspoon white pepper
4 cups chicken broth
1 16-ounce package large frozen peas
Salt and pepper to taste
1 cup heavy cream
Croutons for garnish

In a medium saucepan, sauté lettuce,
onion and parsley in butter until
onions are translucent and lettuce is
wilted. Add curry, flour and white
pepper; cook about 3 minutes. Add
chicken broth and bring to a boil; add
peas and bring to another boil, then
lower to simmer for 30-35 minutes or
until the peas are thoroughly cooked.
Remove from heat and purée until
smooth in food processor. Soup can be
refrigerated or frozen at this point.

To serve, reheat gently and add heavy
cream. Garnish with croutons.

Serves 6

Cauliflower Bisque

4 tablespoons butter
1 cup sliced leeks, rinsed well
1 cup sliced mushrooms
3 tablespoons flour
3 cups chicken broth
1 cup cauliflower florets
1 cup light cream
1 cup grated Jarlsberg cheese

In a large saucepan, sauté leeks and
mushrooms in butter until tender.
Add flour and cook, stirring until bubbling. Remove from heat and gradually
blend in chicken broth. Return to heat;
cook and stir until smooth and thick.
Add cauliflower; reduce heat and simmer 15 minutes or until cauliflower is
tender. Blend in cream and cheese and
cook over low heat until cheese is
melted.

Serves 6

*The cheese is the key to this favorite soup.
Prepare it once and you will prepare it
again and again.*

Sweet Potato Leek Soup

2 tablespoons butter
1 red onion, diced
1 clove garlic, minced
1 bunch leeks, white part only, sliced
    and washed well
2 pounds sweet potatoes, peeled and
    cut into cubes
3 cups chicken broth
1 teaspoon nutmeg
2 teaspoons salt
1/2 teaspoon cayenne pepper
1 cup light cream
1/4 cup chopped chives

In a large saucepan, sauté onions, garlic
and leeks in butter over moderate heat
until soft. Stir in the potatoes and cook
for 5 minutes. Add the broth, nutmeg,
salt and cayenne and simmer until potatoes are tender, about 20 minutes. In
a food processor or blender, process the
soup in batches using quick on-off
turns to produce a textured purée. Stir
in the cream and heat through. Season
to taste. Garnish with fresh chives.

Serves 6

Spinach Soup with Cheese Froth

1/2 pound fresh spinach, chopped
1 cup chicken broth
1 cup sour cream
1 teaspoon cornstarch
1/2 cup light cream
1 teaspoon salt
1/2 teaspoon pepper
1/4 teaspoon nutmeg
Pinch cayenne pepper

Cheese Froth
1/2 cup heavy cream, chilled
1/4 cup grated Swiss cheese
Grated nutmeg to taste

Simmer spinach and broth for 5
minutes. Stir sour cream and
cornstarch together and stir into
spinach mixture. Heat and stir to keep
smooth. Add cream and seasonings. Be
careful not to boil.

Cheese Froth: Whip heavy cream until
soft peaks form; fold in cheese and
nutmeg.

To serve, pour warm soup into
individual bowls and top with a dollop
of cheese froth. Place under broiler
until bubbly and lightly browned.

Serves 4

Harvest Chowder

3 tablespoons butter
1 medium onion, chopped
1 cup sliced carrots
1/2 cup sliced celery
2 cups potatoes, peeled and cut into
    1-inch cubes
1 16-ounce can tomatoes
2 cups milk
1 1/2 teaspoons Worcestershire sauce
2 beef bouillon cubes
2 cups grated sharp Cheddar cheese
2 tablespoons chopped parsley
Salt and pepper to taste

Melt butter in stock pot over medium
heat. Stir in the vegetables and simmer
until vegetables are tender. Add milk
gradually, then mix in the
Worcestershire sauce and bouillon
cubes. Simmer 30-40 minutes over low
heat. Stir in cheese and parsley. Season
to taste with salt and pepper.

Serves 8

Fresh Asparagus Bisque

8 slices bacon, cut into small pieces

1 pound fresh asparagus, dry ends
   removed
3 medium scallions

3¼ cups milk
1 tablespoon cornstarch
1 tablespoon butter
Salt to taste
1/3 cup mayonnaise
1 cup grated Swiss cheese for garnish

Sauté bacon pieces until crisp; drain well and set aside.

Cut asparagus and scallions into 1-inch pieces. Boil in water to cover until barely tender, about 10 minutes. Drain. Purée in food processor and set aside.

Heat 3 cups of the milk and add cornstarch which has been blended with remaining 1/4 cup milk. Stir constantly until thickened. Add butter. Salt to taste. Add mayonnaise and asparagus purée; stir until blended. Continue stirring until heated through. Remove from heat.

Serve in warmed soup bowls. Garnish with grated cheese and bacon pieces.

Serves 6

Fresh Vegetables and Cream

3/4 cup butter
3/4 cup chopped onion
1½ cups peeled, diced tomato
3/4 cup diced carrot
3/4 cup green beans
3/4 cup chopped broccoli
3/4 cup finely chopped leek
3/4 cup finely chopped zucchini
1 clove garlic, minced
1½ teaspoons sugar
Salt and pepper to taste
6 cups chicken broth
1/2 cup heavy cream
Sour cream for garnish
Parsley for garnish

Melt butter in a soup pot. Sauté onion 1 to 2 minutes. Reduce heat to medium and add all ingredients except broth and cream. Cook 20-25 minutes, stirring occasionally. Add broth and bring to a boil over medium heat. Reduce heat and simmer 10 minutes. Cool slightly (5 to 10 minutes). Purée in food processor in batches. (Soup can be frozen at this point.) Return puréed soup to pot. Stir in cream. Heat. Garnish with a dollop of sour cream and a sprig of fresh parsley.

Serves 6-8

Summer Garden Soup with Pesto

2½ cups peeled, diced potatoes
2 cups diced carrots
2 cups diced yellow onions
12 cups water
1 cup fresh green beans, cut up
1 cup canned canellini (white beans),
   drained
1/2 cup chopped red or green pepper
1/2 cup diced zucchini or yellow squash
1/2 cup snow peas
1/2 cup small pasta or broken spaghetti
1/2 teaspoon saffron threads
Freshly ground pepper

4 cloves garlic
4 tablespoons tomato paste
1/2 cup fresh basil leaves
1/2 cup freshly grated Parmesan cheese
2 tablespoons fresh parsley
1/4 cup olive oil

Simmer potatoes, carrots and onions in water for about 45 minutes. Add vegetables, pasta and seasonings and boil slowly until green vegetables are tender. Add hot water if soup is too thick. Season.

Place garlic, tomato paste, basil, Parmesan cheese and parsley in food processor and process until roughly ground. Pour oil in gradually until basil pesto is formed.

To serve, ladle soup into a warmed tureen. Thin pesto with 1/2 cup of soup. Return to tureen.

Serves 6-8

White Gazpacho

3 cups chicken broth
3 medium cucumbers, peeled, seeded
   and cubed
3 cups sour cream
3 tablespoons white vinegar
2 teaspoons garlic salt
1/2 teaspoon celery salt
1/4 teaspoon white pepper
1/2 cup scallions, sliced with green tops
1/2 cup minced fresh parsley
2 tomatoes, peeled, seeded and diced
1/2 cup chopped fresh mushrooms
1/2 cup slivered almonds, toasted

Put 1 cup chicken broth in food processor with cucumbers and purée until
smooth. Combine with remaining
broth. Add sour cream, vinegar, garlic
salt, celery salt and white pepper. Chill.
Add scallions, parsley, tomatoes and
mushrooms just before serving, saving
a few scallions and parsley for garnish.
Top each serving with toasted almonds.

Serves 6-8

Orange and Tomato Soup

3 tablespoons butter
4 medium onions, finely chopped
1 medium potato, peeled and finely
   chopped
4 cloves garlic, minced
1 16-ounce can tomatoes
Juice and grated rind of one medium
   orange
1 can chicken broth
1/2 cup heavy cream
1 tablespoon sugar
Salt and pepper to taste

In a large saucepan, sauté onion, potato
and garlic in butter until soft. Add
tomatoes, orange juice, orange rind and
broth; simmer 30 minutes. Process in a
food processor or blender until smooth.
Just before serving, add cream, sugar
and seasonings. Serve warm.

Serves 6

Cold Tomato Cream

1 tablespoon butter
1 onion, chopped
6 tomatoes, peeled, seeded and
   chopped
3/4 cup chicken broth
1/2 teaspoon salt
1/2 teaspoon thyme
1/2 teaspoon sugar
1 tablespoon tomato paste
3/4 cup heavy cream
1/4 cup sour cream
Juice of 1 lime
Salt and pepper to taste
Lemon or lime slices for garnish

In a medium saucepan, melt butter and
sauté onions over moderate heat until
clear and soft. Add tomatoes, chicken
broth, salt, thyme, sugar and tomato
paste and simmer, covered, for 15 minutes. Let cool and process in a blender
or food processor until smooth. Add
cream and sour cream and process. Add
lime juice and season to taste. Chill
for 2 hours or more. Garnish with thin
lemon or lime slices.

Serves 4

Beet and Horseradish Soup

2 pounds beets, scrubbed and trimmed,
  leaving 2" stems intact
1 large onion, chopped
3 tablespoons unsalted butter
1¼ cups dry red wine
1/4 cup fresh lemon juice
2½ tablespoons drained bottled
  horseradish
1 large carrot, grated
1 cup sour cream
1¼ teaspoons salt
1 teaspoon white pepper
12 lemon slices
Sour cream for garnish
Grated onion for garnish
Grated carrot for garnish

In a kettle, cover beets with 3 inches of cold water; bring to boil and simmer the beets, covered, for 15-35 minutes or until tender. Transfer beets with slotted spoon to colander, reserving cooking liquid, and let them cool until they can be handled. Slip off skins and cut into 1-inch pieces. Remove kettle from heat and let the reserved liquid settle for 15 minutes.

In a large saucepan, cook onion in butter over moderate heat, stirring until golden. Ladle out 3½ cups of the reserved cooking liquid without disturbing the sediment in the bottom of the kettle. Stir it into the onion mixture with the wine, lemon juice, horseradish, grated carrot and beets. Simmer the mixture, whisking, for 5 minutes.

In blender or food processor, process the mixture in batches until smooth. Return it to the pan and whisk in 1 cup of sour cream. Season with salt and pepper and heat over moderate heat, stirring until it is hot, but do not allow it to boil.

Serve hot or cold. Garnish with lemon slices, sour cream, grated onion and grated carrot.

Serves 6

For a dramatic presentation, serve in oversized glass balloon goblets and pipe sour cream artistically on top.

Zucchini Cream

4 medium zucchini, quartered and
  sliced
2 15-ounce cans chicken broth
1 bunch scallions, chopped
1 teaspoon salt
1 teaspoon pepper
Fresh dill to taste
2 8-ounce packages cream cheese
1 cup sour cream
1 bunch fresh chives, finely chopped

Place zucchini, chicken broth, scallions, salt, pepper and dill in a medium saucepan. Cook over low heat for 30 minutes. Remove from heat and purée mixture in food processor until smooth.

In a separate bowl, blend cream cheese and sour cream until smooth. Add to the purée and reheat gently. At this point, the soup may be served warm and garnished with fresh chives or refrigerated overnight and served chilled the next day.

Serves 6-8

Perfect for a blanket party. Simply pour into a thermos and pack with your picnic of Tangy Rye Sticks, apples and Orange Oatmeal Cookies.

Chilled Cherry Soup

1½ pounds fresh sour cherries, pitted
1/3 cup sugar
2¼ teaspoons cornstarch
1/4 teaspoon salt
1/4 teaspoon nutmeg
1/4 teaspoon cinnamon
Grated rind of one large orange
    (approximately 1/2 cup)
1/2 cup red Bordeaux wine

Place cherries in food processor. Process until finely ground. Place contents in a food mill and press through into a saucepan. Add all remaining ingredients except the wine and bring to a boil. Stir constantly. Remove from heat and stir in wine. Chill at least 24 hours before serving.

If fresh cherries are not available, drained canned sour cherries can be substituted.

Serves 4

Cold Strawberry Soup

1 quart fresh strawberries, hulled and
    coarsely puréed
2 cups freshly squeezed orange juice
6 tablespoons honey
16 ounces plain yogurt
Fresh strawberries for garnish

In a large bowl, whisk together strawberry purée, orange juice and honey. Gently stir in yogurt until blended. Chill at least 4 hours before serving. Serve in chilled bowls topped with a strawberry.

Serves 6-8

A chilled fruit soup is especially welcome in the summer. An ideal first course for a luncheon or a light ending to a late supper.

Chilled Cantaloupe Soup

6 medium cantaloupes, halved and
    seeded
1/2 cup dry sherry
1/2 cup sugar
1½ cups freshly squeezed orange juice
Mint leaves

Scoop pulp from each cantaloupe, leaving shells 1/2-inch thick. Cut a thin slice from bottom of each shell, being careful not to cut a hole in the shell. This enables shell to sit level so that it can be used as a serving bowl.

Combine cantaloupe pulp, dry sherry, sugar and orange juice in a food processor or blender. Process until smooth. Chill thoroughly. Serve soup in cantaloupe shells or in large stemmed glasses. Garnish with mint leaves.

Serves 12

Salads

Mixed Reds

1 head red leaf lettuce
1/2 head radicchio
1/4 cup shredded red cabbage
2 radishes, thinly sliced
3 tablespoons pomegranate seeds

Dressing
2 tablespoons red wine vinegar
1 tablespoon red raspberry vinegar
4 tablespoons light olive oil
1/2 teaspoon Dijon mustard
Salt and pepper to taste

Red nasturtiums for decoration

Wash, dry and shred lettuce into bite-size pieces. Split radicchio leaves into thirds. Combine all salad ingredients and sprinkle with pomegranate seeds.

Dressing: Whisk dressing ingredients together and toss with salad just before serving. Separate evenly onto 6 salad plates and decorate with nasturtiums, if available.

Serves 6

Panzanella Bread Crab Salad

1/2 pound (1/2 large loaf) crusty Italian style bread
2 large tomatoes, diced
1/3 cup minced red onion
1/2 cup pitted black olives
1 bunch basil, cut in strips
3 cloves garlic, minced
8 ounces fresh crab
1/3 cup olive oil
2 tablespoons red wine vinegar
Salt and pepper to taste
Chives to garnish

Tear bread into small bits. Sprinkle with water until moist but not soggy. Add all vegetables and herbs and mix well with hands. Add crab. Mix oil and vinegar. Toss lightly with salad, then add salt and pepper to taste. Garnish with long chives crossed on top.

Serves 6

White and Wild Rice Salad

3 cups cooked wild rice
3 cups cooked white rice
1½ pounds seedless green grapes, halved
1 14-ounce can artichoke hearts, drained and quartered
3/4 cup chopped parsley
1 cup toasted pecans
1 pint fresh raspberries for garnish

Raspberry Vinaigrette Dressing
1/2 cup light olive oil or safflower oil
3/4 cup raspberry vinegar
1/4 cup fresh tarragon or 1 tablespoon dried
Salt and pepper to taste

Cook rice according to package directions. A good quality slow-cooking rice is recommended. Cool. Add grapes, artichoke hearts, parsley and pecans.

Dressing: Combine and whisk together the oil, vinegar, tarragon, salt and pepper.

Dress rice salad to taste with dressing. Garnish with fresh raspberries for color.

Serves 10-12

Contributed by Culinary Concepts

Shrimp Bombay

1 pound large or medium shrimp
3 bay leaves
8 whole cloves
3 peppercorns
1/2 cup shelled pistachio nuts
1 tablespoon minced fresh ginger
4 tablespoons lemon juice
2 teaspoons curry powder
1/2 teaspoon hot pepper sauce
    (optional)
1/4 teaspoon ground coriander
1 teaspoon ground cumin
3 scallions, minced
5 tablespoons vegetable oil
1 tablespoon orange juice
1/2 pound snow peas, blanched or
    1 head romaine lettuce

In a medium saucepan, cover shrimp with water. Add bay leaves, cloves and peppercorns and bring to a boil. Remove shrimp when firm and pink, about 1 to 2 minutes. Allow shrimp to cool; peel. Combine shrimp and nuts in a bowl and set aside.

In food processor, process ginger, lemon juice, curry, hot pepper sauce, coriander, cumin, scallions, oil and orange juice for 30 seconds. Pour over shrimp and nuts. Chill. Arrange on large platter with wreath of snow peas or lettuce.

Serves 4

Shrimp Salad with Avocado

2 pounds medium shrimp
1/2 medium lemon, sliced
1 teaspoon salt

Dressing
1/2 cup mayonnaise
1/4 cup sour cream
1 tablespoon lemon juice
1 tablespoon capers
1/2 cup finely chopped scallions
1/2 cup finely chopped celery
1 tablespoon minced garlic
1/2 teaspoon dry mustard

Small head Bibb lettuce
2 ripe avocados
1/2 medium lemon
Salt and pepper to taste

Bring large pot of water to boil. Add lemon slices and 1 teaspoon salt. Add shrimp; return water to boil and allow shrimp to cook 1 to 2 minutes, stirring. Drain shrimp in colander and rinse under cold water. Chill. Peel and devein.

Dressing: Whisk together all dressing ingredients in medium-size bowl.

Pour dressing over shrimp. Chill at least 4 hours, allowing flavors to blend. Serve on leaves of Bibb lettuce and garnish with avocado slices; or, cut avocado in half, fill with shrimp salad and place on Bibb lettuce. Use other half of lemon to lightly sprinkle avocado. Salt and pepper to taste.

Serves 4

Shrimp Salad in Sesame Shells

2 pounds medium shrimp, cooked,
    peeled and deveined
1 cup finely chopped mushrooms
1/3 cup chopped scallions
1 clove garlic, minced
1/4 teaspoon cayenne pepper
1/2 cup mayonnaise
1 tablespoon fresh lemon juice
1/4 cup chopped parsley

Shells
3 ounces Neufchatel cheese, softened
1/2 cup butter, softened
1 cup flour
1/2 cup sesame seeds
Baking shells

Combine shrimp with mushrooms, scallions, garlic, cayenne pepper, mayonnaise, lemon juice and parsley, stirring after each addition.

Shells: Preheat oven to 325 degrees. Cover baking shells with foil. Carefully press foil to insure that pastry makes the shape of a shell when added. Cream together Neufchatel cheese and butter. Add flour and sesame seeds. Mix well. Separate dough mixture into 2-inch balls. Roll out each 2-inch ball of dough to 1/8-inch thickness and press into foil covered shell. Prick all over with a fork. Trim edges and place on a baking sheet. Bake for approximately 20 minutes. Let cool before removing pastry.

Just before serving, fill pastry shells with shrimp.

Serves 6-8

The Breakfast Salad

3 tablespoons light olive oil
1½ cups cubed French bread, lightly
    toasted
3 heads romaine lettuce
6 eggs

Dressing
14 slices bacon
2 tablespoons safflower oil
2 tablespoons finely minced onion
2 tablespoons red wine vinegar
Salt and pepper to taste

In medium skillet, heat olive oil. Add
toasted bread cubes and sauté until
crisp and golden; set aside. Wash and
dry romaine; tear into bite-size pieces;
set aside. Hard boil eggs; cool. Shell
and cut in half lengthwise; set aside.

Dressing: In large saucepan, fry bacon
until crisp; crumble and set aside.
Drain all but 3 tablespoons of
drippings from pan. Add safflower oil
and onion; cook until onion is lightly
browned. Add vinegar, salt and pepper
to taste.

In medium bowl, combine lettuce,
croutons and bacon. Toss with enough
dressing to coat. To serve, arrange salad
greens evenly on 6 salad plates. Place
two egg halves in center of greens and
dribble with a small amount of
dressing. Pour remaining dressing into
a small pitcher to be served separately.

Serves 6

Spaghetti Squash Salad

1 medium spaghetti squash
1/4 pound mushrooms, thinly sliced
1/2 cup julienne red pepper
1/2 cup julienne green pepper
1 4-ounce can pitted black olives,
    drained and sliced
2 medium ripe avocados, pitted, peeled
    and sliced into crescents
1 head red leaf lettuce, washed and
    trimmed

Champagne Vinaigrette with Avocado
3/4 cup avocado or safflower oil
1/4 cup champagne vinegar
2-3 cloves garlic, minced
1 teaspoon minced fresh oregano
1 teaspoon minced fresh basil
1 teaspoon dry mustard
1 teaspoon Worcestershire sauce
Salt and freshly ground pepper

Dressing: Whisk together oil, vinegar,
garlic, herbs, mustard, Worcestershire
sauce and salt and pepper to taste.
Refrigerate overnight to allow flavors to
blend.

Preheat oven to 350 degrees. Prick the
squash in several places, place in a
baking pan and set in the oven for
about 1½ hours, or until the flesh is
tender. Cool. Cut in half. Remove
seeds and using a fork, shred squash
into strands. Combine in medium bowl
with mushrooms, red and green
peppers, olives and avocado. Just prior
to serving, toss with vinaigrette and
arrange on a bed of red leaf lettuce.

Serves 6

Vegetable Medley

2 cups green beans, blanched and cut
    on an angle
1 cup diced celery
1 cup chopped green pepper
1 cup chopped red pepper
1 cup sliced mushrooms
1 cup broccoli florets
1 cup cauliflower florets
1/2 cup chopped onion

Marinade
3/4 cup sugar
1/2 teaspoon pepper
1 teaspoon salt
1/2 cup vegetable oil
3/4 cup vinegar
1 teaspoon celery seed

Combine vegetables in a medium bowl.
In a small saucepan, combine marinade
ingredients and bring to a boil over
medium heat, stirring occasionally.
Pour marinade over vegetables, stirring
gently to blend well. Cover and chill
overnight.

Serves 8

*An array of color with a sweet surprise is
a perfect complement to Charcoal Shrimp
with Scallion Butter.*

Wheat Berries du Soleil

2 cups dry wheat berries (can be found in health food stores or specialty grocery stores)
7 cups water

Dressing
1/4 cup orange juice
1/4 cup pineapple juice
1/4 cup safflower oil
2 tablespoons orange peel, grated
1 tablespoon lemon peel, grated
1/4 cup chopped fresh basil or
    1 tablespoon dried
1/4 cup chopped fresh tarragon or
    1 tablespoon dried
1 tablespoon freshly ground pepper
1 tablespoon sugar
1 tablespoon chopped fresh sage or
    1 1/4 teaspoons dried

1 fresh pineapple, chopped
1 11-ounce can mandarin oranges
1 small red pepper, julienne
1 cup frozen green peas, thawed
6-8 scallions, chopped
2 cups cashew halves

Garnish
1/2 cup sour cream
1/2 cup mayonnaise
1/4 cup chopped fresh dill or
    1 tablespoon dried
Mandarin oranges
Slivered red pepper

Soak wheat berries in 7 cups water overnight. The next day, boil berries slowly in soaking water for 45-60 minutes in covered pan. Check periodically and add more water if necessary. Wheat berries should be crunchy; do not overcook. Drain, rinse and dry. These fully cooked wheat berries keep up to a week.

Dressing: Combine all ingredients and blend well.

Combine fruits and vegetables with wheat berries. Pour dressing over salad; toss well. Cover and refrigerate for 6 hours or overnight. Drain excess dressing. Just before serving, combine sour cream, mayonnaise and dill. Stir into salad. Garnish with mandarin orange and slivers of red pepper.

Serves 12-16

A unique blend of flavors and textures make this tasty salad a winner.

Wheat Salad with Sherry
Vinaigrette

1 1/2 cups bulgur (cracked wheat)
1 tablespoon vegetable oil
3 1/2 cups boiling water
2 teaspoons salt
1/2 cup kasha (buckwheat groats)
1 egg, lightly beaten
1/3 pound Virginia baked ham, julienne
8-10 scallions, sliced, reserving ends for garnish
2/3 cup olive oil
1/3 cup sherry vinegar
1/4 cup red wine vinegar
Salt and pepper
Small bunch parsley

In a saucepan, toast bulgur in hot oil, stirring frequently, until it begins to crackle (or turns a golden brown). Remove from heat and add 3 cups of boiling water and 1 teaspoon salt. Cover and simmer for approximately 20 minutes or until liquid is absorbed. Set aside.

In a large bowl, mix kasha with half the beaten egg. Pour into saucepan over high heat; toss kasha until egg coating is dry and all grains are separate. Add remaining boiling water and salt. Cover and cook over low heat until liquid is absorbed, approximately 15 minutes. Add to cracked wheat and let cool. Combine ham, scallions, oil, vinegars, salt and pepper to taste and toss with cracked wheat and buckwheat mixtures. Garnish with sprigs of parsley and ends of scallions.

Serves 8

Tomato, Cucumber and Goat Cheese

1 cucumber, thinly sliced
2 or 3 tomatoes, thinly sliced
3 ounces French goat cheese
1 tablespoon chopped fresh oregano
  leaves
4 tablespoons olive oil
2 tablespoons red wine vinegar
Salt and pepper to taste
6 fresh basil leaves
1 green pepper

Sprinkle cucumber with salt. Cover with a plate. Put a weight on the plate and set aside until cucumber is limp. Drain. Make a wreath of tomato and cucumber slices, alternating red and green. Mix chopped oregano into goat cheese and mold into a round cake; place in the center of the vegetable wreath.

Dressing: Mix olive oil, vinegar, salt and pepper and drizzle over vegetables. Snip basil into strips and place on wreath. Cut green pepper into a fan shape by slicing down to the base, being careful not to cut through the base. Spread over the cheese mold to garnish.

Serves 4-5

Japanese Cucumber Salad

1½ cucumbers, pared and sliced into
  paper thin rounds
1 teaspoon salt
1 teaspoon soy sauce
1/2 cup white vinegar
1/4 cup sugar
A few drops sesame oil to taste
1/4 green pepper, slivered
1/2 white onion, thinly sliced
1/4 pound boiled shrimp, cut in half
  lengthwise (optional)
Sesame seeds (optional)

Sprinkle cucumber with salt. Let cucumber drain into bowl in refrigerator overnight. Make dressing by combining soy sauce, vinegar, sugar and sesame seed oil. Just before serving, gently mix together cucumber, green pepper and onion. Add shrimp. Pour dressing over salad. Sprinkle with sesame seeds.

Serves 6

Broccoli Salad

1 large bunch broccoli, finely chopped
1/2 cup dark raisins
1 medium red onion, finely chopped
1 large carrot, finely grated
8 slices bacon, cooked crisp and
  crumbled

Dressing
1/2 cup mayonnaise
1/4 cup red wine vinegar
1 tablespoon poppy seeds
2½ tablespoons sugar

Combine broccoli, raisins, onion and carrot in a medium size bowl.

Dressing: Whisk together mayonnaise, red wine vinegar, poppy seeds and sugar.

Thoroughly coat broccoli mixture with dressing. Chill. Just prior to serving, add bacon to broccoli salad.

Serves 4-6

Warm Scallop Salad with Saffron Vinaigrette

6 cups baby greens (arugula, chervil, chickweed, dandelion and/or oak leaf, all available at specialty produce stores)
24 large fresh sea scallops, sliced in half crosswise
3 tablespoons light olive oil

Dressing
2 large pinches saffron threads
4 tablespoons white wine vinegar
4 tablespoons water
1/2 cup light olive oil, plus extra for salad
2 tablespoons finely chopped shallots
Salt and pepper

Dressing: Over gentle heat, infuse saffron in vinegar and water. Simmer until liquid is reduced by half. Add this to oil with the shallots and season with salt and pepper.

Arrange baby greens evenly among 8 salad plates. Dress the greens with a sprinkle of oil, salt and freshly ground pepper.

In a large non-stick skillet, briskly cook scallops in olive oil, approximately 45 seconds each side, or until golden and just cooked through. Put aside and cover to keep warm. Deglaze pan with the dressing, adding a bit of water. Place 6 scallop rounds on each plate around the greens. Top with hot vinaigrette.

Serves 8

Warm Spinach, Arugula and Basil Salad

1 pound fresh spinach
1 bunch arugula
18 basil leaves
1/3 cup toasted pine nuts
1/4 teaspoon salt
1/3 teaspoon pepper
1 julienne red pepper, roasted and peeled
3 ounces French goat cheese

Dressing
1/2 cup extra virgin olive oil
1/4 cup balsamic vinegar

Wash and thoroughly dry greens. In a large bowl, combine the greens, pine nuts, salt and pepper.

Dressing: In a sauté pan, heat oil and vinegar until very hot (vinegar will begin to boil).

To serve, toss the warm dressing with the greens, pine nuts, salt and pepper. Divide among 6 salad plates and garnish with strips of roasted pepper. Crumble goat cheese over each salad.

Serves 6

Contributed by Rollers Restaurant

Salad of Warm Wild Mushrooms

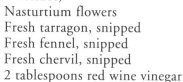

8 ounces fresh wild mushrooms (chanterelles, ceps, oysters)
3 ounces walnut or hazelnut oil
1 clove garlic, peeled and finely diced
1 shallot, peeled and finely diced
Salt and freshly ground pepper
3 sorts of firm young lettuce (red chicory, curly leaf endive, lamb's lettuce)
Nasturtium flowers
Fresh tarragon, snipped
Fresh fennel, snipped
Fresh chervil, snipped
2 tablespoons red wine vinegar

Clean mushrooms and cut into pieces. In medium saucepan, sauté shallot and garlic in a small amount of the oil for about 3 minutes; do not brown. Add mushrooms and continue to sauté until tender. Season to taste with salt and pepper.

Wash and pat dry lettuce and place with nasturtiums and snipped herbs in a large warm bowl. Pour hot mushrooms with shallot and garlic and pan juices into the leaves. Heat remainder of the oil and add this to the mixture. Bubble up the vinegar in the hot pan, reduce by half, and pour onto salad greens. Season again with salt and pepper and toss well.

Serves 6

Cold Duck Salad with
Orange Zest

1 duck, approximately 4 pounds
2 celery stalks, chopped
1 small onion, chopped
5 garlic cloves
1 tablespoon thyme
1 tablespoon sage
2 oranges
2 4-ounce packages alfalfa shoots
1 8-ounce can water chestnuts, drained
    and sliced

Dressing
6 tablespoons orange juice
2 tablespoons lemon juice
1½ teaspoons Dijon mustard
6 tablespoons pecan oil
1/8 teaspoon thyme
1/4 teaspoon fennel

Day Before: Stuff cavity of duck with celery, onion and garlic cloves. Rub thyme and sage into skin. Place in roasting bag and make six 1/2-inch cuts for steam to escape. Roast 2 hours at 325 degrees. Slow roasting keeps it moist. Peel oranges with sharp knife, taking care to remove membrane along with rind. Cut peel of 1 orange into 1½-inch julienne strips. (Save other orange peel for garnish.) Blanch orange peel strips in boiling water for 5 minutes. Remove duck from oven. Remove celery, onion and garlic cloves from cavity. Save garlic. Remove skin from duck. Spread garlic, like butter, over duck. Put into refrigerator to cool.

Dressing: Combine all dressing ingredients. Whisk until thoroughly blended. Refrigerate.

To assemble, cut duck into sand dollar size pieces. Slice oranges. Pile alfalfa shoots on platter. Center garnish of reserved orange peel. Arrange duck and orange slices alternately around garnish. Sprinkle sliced water chestnuts and julienne strips of orange peel over duck and orange slices. Just before serving, drizzle dressing over all. Pour extra dressing into a small pitcher to be served separately.

Serves 6

A flair of the unusual that can be prepared ahead for a special salad buffet. Serve with cold Pasta Primavera, Sunrise Salad and a basket of warm Southern Dinner Rolls.

Fresh Fruit with Lemon Sherry
Dressing

1/3 cup dry sherry
1/3 cup fresh lemon juice
3 tablespoons sugar
1 cup strawberries, quartered
3/4 cup blueberries
3 cups peeled, sliced peaches or papaya
3/4 cup seedless green grapes, halved
1/2 fresh pineapple, peeled, cored, cut
    in small wedges
1 red apple, unpeeled, cored and cut
    into small wedges
2 kiwis or prickly pears, peeled and
    sliced
1 head romaine lettuce
6-10 whole strawberries
Mint leaves

Combine sherry, lemon juice and sugar; whisk until sugar dissolves. Combine fruit, coat with dressing and toss gently. Refrigerate.

To serve, line 6 dessert plates with romaine lettuce leaves. Divide fruit evenly among the plates. Garnish with whole strawberries and mint leaves.

Serves 6

Grilled Chicken and Greens

1/4 cup honey
1/4 cup Dijon mustard
2 chicken breasts, split

Dressing
3/4 cup raspberry vinegar
1/3 cup champagne vinegar
1 large lemon
2/3 cup safflower oil
3 tablespoons honey
Salt and freshly ground pepper

1 head red leaf lettuce
1 bunch fresh watercress, trimmed
1 head radicchio
1 small bunch Belgian endive
1 small bunch seedless red or green
   grapes
2 small Granny Smith apples
1 large lemon
1 pint raspberries

3 ounces French goat cheese
4 ounces pine nuts

One or two days ahead, thoroughly blend honey and mustard. Pour over chicken breasts and marinate overnight in the refrigerator. Turn chicken several times. Grill over slow fire, 7-10 minutes each side. Do not overcook. Cool, shred chicken into bite-size pieces; do not cube; refrigerate.

Rinse and pat dry salad greens. Tear into bite-size pieces. Use slightly more red leaf or radicchio than trimmed watercress and endive. Refrigerate.

Slice grapes in half. Slice apples thinly and coat with the juice of 1 lemon to preserve freshness. Rinse raspberries. Refrigerate.

Dressing: Combine vinegars, juice of 1 lemon, oil and honey. Whisk. Add salt and pepper to taste. Shake well and refrigerate.

Shortly before serving, combine chicken, lettuces and fruits. Toss with vinaigrette. Divide evenly among 6-8 salad plates. Top with crumbled cheese and sprinkle with pine nuts.

Serves 6-8

Perfect for entertaining as the grilled chicken, lettuces, fruits and dressing can all be prepared ahead.

Oriental Chicken Salad

4 boneless, skinless chicken breast
   halves
2 cups chicken broth
1 2x4-inch slice ginger root
5 scallions, chopped
1/2 package won ton wrappers
2 heads romaine lettuce, washed, dried
1 8-ounce can sliced water chestnuts
3 tablespoons chopped parsley
2 scallions, sliced
1/2 pound fresh snow peas
2 tablespoons sesame seeds, toasted

Dressing
4 tablespoons sugar
1 teaspoon salt
1/3 cup safflower oil
1/2 teaspoon coarsely ground pepper
5 tablespoons rice wine vinegar
3 tablespoons soy sauce

Simmer chicken breasts in broth with ginger root and scallions just until tender. Remove chicken with slotted spoon; shred into bite-size pieces.

Cut each won ton into 4 triangles. Fry in hot oil until golden brown. Set aside.

Dressing: Combine all dressing ingredients. Whisk until thoroughly blended.

Combine the chicken, lettuce, water chestnuts, parsley, scallions and snow peas. Toss with dressing. Sprinkle with sesame seeds and won tons.

Serves 8-12

Belgian Endive and Beet Salad

2 large heads Belgian endive
2 fresh medium beets
8 sprigs fresh lemon basil

Dressing
5 leaves fresh lemon basil
1/2 cup lemon juice
1/2 cup safflower oil
1 teaspoon Dijon mustard
Salt and freshly ground pepper

Trim endive and shred into bite-size pieces. Divide among 4 plates. Cook beets until tender; peel and julienne. Arrange over endive. Decorate each plate with 2 fresh sprigs of lemon basil. Drizzle dressing over salad.

Dressing: Mince basil leaves and combine in a jar with lemon juice, oil and mustard. Add salt and pepper to taste. Shake until ingredients are well mixed.

Serves 4

A simple but smashing beginning to a dinner of Minted Grilled Lamb Chops and Untamed Rice.

Greens and Sherry Mustard

Dressing

2 heads Bibb lettuce
2 bunches dandelion greens
1 small bunch arugula
1 small bunch watercress

Sherry Mustard Vinaigrette
1/2 cup light olive oil
4 tablespoons sherry wine vinegar
2 teaspoons Dijon mustard
1 tablespoon fresh chervil leaves
Salt and freshly ground pepper

Wash, dry and trim salad greens. Tear into bite-size pieces. Arrange on 6 salad plates. Coat lightly with vinaigrette.

Dressing: Whisk together oil, vinegar, mustard and chervil leaves. Salt and pepper to taste.

Serves 6

Blue Cheese Potato Salad

4 pounds small red potatoes, unpeeled

Dressing
1/4 cup cider vinegar
2 tablespoons tarragon vinegar
2 tablespoons Dijon mustard
Salt and pepper to taste
2 tablespoons minced fresh tarragon
1/4 cup sesame oil
1/2 cup light olive oil
1/4 cup minced shallots
2 tablespoons minced parsley

1/2 cup blue cheese
1/2 cup heavy cream
12 slices bacon, cooked crisp and
   crumbled
3 tablespoons minced chives

Boil potatoes until tender; do not overcook. While potatoes are cooking, prepare dressing. Cool potatoes slightly and cut into 1/4-inch slices. Place potatoes in large bowl and mix in 1/2 cup of dressing.

Dressing: Mix vinegars, mustard, salt, pepper and tarragon in small bowl or food processor. Whisk in or process oils in a thin steady stream. Stir in shallots and minced parsley. Reserve.

When ready to serve, whisk cheese and heavy cream into remaining dressing and pour over all in serving bowl. Sprinkle with bacon and chives. Gently mix all before serving. Serve warm or at room temperature.

Serves 6-8

Basil Dill Vinaigrette

1 egg
1 1/4 cups safflower oil
1/4 cup red wine vinegar
1 clove garlic, minced
1 teaspoon dried basil
1 teaspoon dried dill
1 teaspoon salt
1/4 teaspoon black pepper

In a food processor, whisk egg. Add oil in a thin stream to make a mayonnaise-like dressing. Add the vinegar, garlic, basil, dill, salt and pepper. Store in the refrigerator for up to 2 weeks.

Yields 1 1/2 cups

Lime Ginger Dressing

3/4 cup light olive oil
1/4 cup fresh lime juice
2 tablespoons honey
1/4 teaspoon ground ginger
Pinch cayenne pepper
Salt and freshly ground pepper

Whisk together oil, lime juice, honey, ginger and cayenne. Add salt and pepper to taste. Refrigerate.

Yields 1 cup

Walnut Dressing with Matag

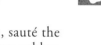

3 shallots, peeled
2 tablespoons sherry vinegar
1/2 teaspoon salt
1/4 teaspoon pepper
1/2 cup extra virgin olive oil
3/4 teaspoon walnut oil
35 toasted walnut halves
1/2 pound Matag blue cheese

In a moderately hot saucepan, sauté the shallots until they begin to turn golden, about 5-7 minutes. Let shallots cool and chop them finely.

Combine in a small bowl vinegar, salt, pepper and shallots. Add oil in a thin stream until it is emulsified.

Pour dressing over greens of choice and toss well with walnuts and blue cheese.

Yields 3/4 cup

Called the "Athens of America" in colonial times, Philadelphia has long been a major center of commerce, learning and the arts. It is still home to some of the oldest and finest scientific museums, notably the Academy of Natural Sciences and the Franklin Institute.

In music, Leopold Stokowski, Eugene Ormandy and Riccardo Muti have led the Philadelphia Orchestra to international fame and stature. The Opera Company is well-known for its annual finals of the Luciano Pavarotti International Voice Competition. And who can look at Philadelphia's musical past without recognizing it as the home of American Bandstand? The Pennsylvania Ballet Company, theatres such as the Forrest, Zellerbach and Walnut Street, have enhanced the city's reputation for world-class cultural activity.

In the visual arts, the works of Mary Cassatt, the Andrew Wyeth family and Thomas Eakins provide some of the most sensitive perspectives on local people and places. And the charm of Philadelphia is preserved in its lovingly restored architecture — three centuries of style and substance, industry and exuberance.

It is said that writer Edgar Allen Poe's years in Philadelphia were among his most successful and happy. Though elaborate entertaining was beyond his means, Poe and his wife enjoyed sharing these times with friends. They welcomed friends simply with sliced peaches from their backyard tree.

In this same spirit, we invite you into the bounty of Philadelphia's culture and the hospitality of our homes.

*Founded in 1812,
the Academy of Natural
Sciences is America's
first natural history
museum.*

*The constantly moving
giant pendulum dominates
the four floors of the
Franklin Institute, the
science museum named for
Benjamin Franklin.*

*The Philadelphia Museum
of Art resembles a
Greek temple and contains
over 200 galleries and over
500,000 works of art.*

*The Rodin Museum
on the Parkway houses the
largest collection of
Auguste Rodin's work
outside of Paris.*

*Pennsylvania Academy of
Fine Arts, the oldest
museum and school in
America, has fostered some
of the country's finest
artists.*

*The main branch of the
Free Library of Philadelphia
features an impressive
collection of rare books among
its over two million
volumes.*

*The Academy of Music is
America's oldest musical
auditorium, yet it still boasts
the "perfect" acoustics
designed by Napoleon LeBrun.*

*Theatre has prospered
in Philadelphia with local
theatres staging
Broadway-bound and
original plays as pictured
here at the
Wilma Theatre.*

*A fine example of Greek
revival architecture, the
Fairmount Park
Water Works was built in
1812 and provided water
to the city.*

Seafood

◀ *Apricot Chicken*
◀ ◀ *Brandied Pork Chops*
◀ ◀ ◀ *Swordfish with Tomato Basil Beurre Blanc*

Shrimp with Feta and Ouzo

1 tablespoon olive oil
1 medium yellow onion, chopped
1 clove garlic, minced
1 28-ounce can of peeled plum
    tomatoes, drained well
1 6-ounce can tomato paste
Salt and pepper to taste
1-2 tablespoons capers, drained
1/4 teaspoon sugar
1 tablespoon butter
1 tablespoon olive oil
2 pounds large shrimp, peeled and
    deveined
2 tablespoons cognac
4 tablespoons ouzo
1/4 pound of feta cheese
2 tablespoons chopped fresh parsley

Heat 1 tablespoon of olive oil in
saucepan. Sauté onion and garlic until
lightly browned. Add tomatoes, tomato
paste, salt, pepper, capers and sugar
and cook over moderate heat until
thick, about 30 minutes.

Preheat oven to 425 degrees. Melt
1 tablespoon butter and 1 tablespoon
olive oil in large heavy skillet. Quickly
cook shrimp until they just turn pink,
1 minute or less. Add cognac and ouzo;
heat and flame shrimp. Remove prompt-
ly. Be careful not to overcook the shrimp.
Place shrimp and all the liquid into a
casserole dish. Cover with the tomato
sauce. Crumble feta over sauce. Sprinkle
with parsley and bake until cheese is
thoroughly melted, about 10 minutes.
Serve over fettucine.

Serves 6-8

Gingered Shrimp with Snow Peas

4 scallions, minced
3 tablespoons soy sauce
2 tablespoons white wine vinegar
2 tablespoons minced garlic
4 teaspoons peeled, grated fresh ginger
1 1/2 teaspoons sesame oil
1 1/2 teaspoons sugar
3/4 teaspoon red pepper flakes
1/4 teaspoon salt
1 to 1 1/2 pounds large or jumbo shrimp,
    peeled and deveined
3 tablespoons butter
1/2 pound fresh snow peas, strings
    removed and blanched
Sliced scallions for garnish

In a large bowl, combine the scallions,
soy sauce, vinegar, garlic, ginger, oil,
sugar, red pepper flakes and salt. Mix
well to combine. Pour over shrimp. Let
marinate for up to 3 hours in the
refrigerator. Bring to room
temperature.

Heat a 10-inch sauté pan or wok and
add butter. When butter is melted, add
the shrimp in one layer. Sauté shrimp
on the first side for 3 minutes or until
opaque. Turn shrimp and sauté 1-2
minutes more, until all are opaque. Do
not overcook. Add remaining marinade
and snow peas and heat just until
warm. Serve over rice and garnish with
sliced scallions.

Serves 4

Charcoal Shrimp with Scallion Butter

2 pounds jumbo shrimp
1/3 cup oil
2/3 cup dry white wine
1 tablespoon apple cider vinegar
1 teaspoon salt
1 teaspoon sugar
1/4 teaspoon freshly ground pepper
1 tablespoon minced fresh parsley
2 cloves garlic, minced

Scallion Butter
4 tablespoons butter
1/2 cup lemon juice
Garlic powder to taste
1/4 cup finely chopped scallions,
    including some of the green

Wash shrimp. Do not remove shells. If
desired, remove back vein by splitting
shell with a sharp knife and removing
vein. Place shrimp in a shallow baking
dish. Mix oil, wine, vinegar, salt, sugar,
pepper, parsley and garlic. Pour marinade over shrimp and stir well. Cover
and refrigerate for at least 2 hours, stirring twice.

Preheat broiler or grill. Cook for 5-7
minutes on each side. Serve with a
small dish of the Scallion Butter.

Scallion Butter: Melt butter, add lemon
juice, garlic powder and scallions.

Serves 4-6

Shrimp and Kielbasa Brochettes

Brochette Seasoning
1/4 cup salt
1 tablespoon garlic powder
1 tablespoon freshly ground pepper
1 tablespoon paprika
3/4 teaspoon onion powder
1/4 teaspoon cayenne pepper
1/4 teaspoon dried thyme
1/4 teaspoon dried oregano

Creole Mustard Sauce
1/2 cup dry white vermouth
2 teaspoons white wine vinegar
2 teaspoons chopped shallots
1 cup heavy cream
1/2 teaspoon dried tarragon
3 teaspoons Creole mustard
1 teaspoon Dijon mustard
2 tablespoons unsalted butter
1/4 teaspoon cayenne pepper
Dash salt

16 jumbo shrimp, peeled and deveined
1 pound smoked kielbasa cut into
    1-inch thick pieces
1 large red bell pepper, seeded, cut into
    2-inch squares and parboiled
1 large green bell pepper, seeded, cut
    into 2-inch squares and parboiled
1/4 cup unsalted butter, melted

Brochette Seasoning: Mix together all seasoning ingredients and store in a glass jar. Seasoning can be used on any fish or grilled poultry.

Creole Mustard Sauce: Boil vermouth, vinegar and shallots in a small saucepan until reduced to 4 tablespoons. Add cream and tarragon. Boil until

thickened and reduced to about 2/3 cup. Reduce heat to medium low. Whisk in mustards and cook 30 seconds. Whisk in butter. Season with cayenne and salt. Keep warm.

To Assemble: Alternate shrimp, kielbasa and peppers on 4 skewers. Sprinkle with seasoning mix. Brush with melted butter. Arrange on a preheated grill or broiler pan and cook until shrimp are opaque, about 7 minutes, turning and basting occasionally with butter.

To Serve: Put a serving of white rice on one side of each plate. Spoon sauce onto other side of plate. Slide ingredients off skewers on top of sauce. Serve immediately.

Serves 4

An easy and entertaining supper that can easily be doubled. Offer the frozen Grand Marnier Soufflé for a surprise ending.

Fiery Shrimp Zagreb

Curry Sauce
3 tablespoons butter
4 tablespoons flour
2 cups milk
3 tablespoons curry powder

1 1/2 pounds large shrimp, peeled and
    deveined
4 tablespoons butter
2 tablespoons vegetable oil
1/4 cup brandy, warmed
1/4 cup white wine
2 tablespoons ketchup
1 teaspoon hot pepper sauce
2 tablespoons Worcestershire sauce
1/4 cup sour cream
2 tablespoons lemon juice

Curry Sauce: In a small saucepan, melt butter. Stir in flour. Simmer for 5 minutes. Slowly add milk. Stir constantly until thickened. Blend in curry and set aside.

Clean shrimp. In a 12-inch sauté pan, over medium high heat, melt the butter and oil. Sauté the shrimp until slightly pink and curling. Pour in 1/4 cup of brandy and ignite with a match. Flambé for 30 seconds to 1 minute. Extinguish with 1/4 cup white wine. Reduce liquid by half, stirring frequently. Gradually stir in thickened curry sauce. Add ketchup, hot pepper sauce and Worcestershire. Stirring constantly, add sour cream and lemon juice. Serve immediately over white rice.

Serves 6

Swordfish Croquettes

Batter
3 eggs
1/4 cup flat beer
3/4 cup flour

1½ pounds swordfish
1/4 pound yellow onions, diced
1/4 pound red and green peppers, diced
1 tablespoon garlic powder
2 tablespoons soy sauce
1 tablespoon Dijon mustard
Dash of salt and pepper
Vegetable oil for deep frying

Combine batter ingredients and set aside for 1 hour. Poach swordfish for approximately 10 minutes per inch of thickness. Drain and blot dry. Grind fish in food processor. Place ground swordfish in a bowl and fold in onions, peppers, seasonings and batter.

Heat vegetable oil in a wok or other pan deep enough to hold 3 inches of oil. Drop large spoonfuls, about 2-3 tablespoons, of swordfish mixture into oil and deep fry for 3-4 minutes per side or until thoroughly cooked and golden brown. Serve with tartar or remoulade sauce. Yields 12 croquettes.

Serves 3-4

Contributed by Gourmet Express

Swordfish with Tomato Basil Beurre Blanc

4 swordfish steaks, 1-inch thick
1/2 cup white wine
2 shallots, minced
6 tablespoons white wine vinegar
1/2 cup white wine
3/4 cup cold butter
2 tomatoes, peeled, seeded and chopped
1/2 cup fresh basil, finely sliced

Rinse swordfish steaks, pat dry and place in a shallow glass or ceramic dish. Pour 1/2 cup wine over steaks, cover and set aside.

Place shallots, vinegar and 1/2 cup wine in a 2-quart saucepan. Boil until liquid has been reduced to 1 tablespoon, about 5-7 minutes over medium high heat. Reduce the heat to low and whisk the cold butter into the wine mixture, 1 to 1½ tablespoons at a time. Whisk constantly. Do not let boil. When all butter is whisked in and sauce is creamy and smooth, add the tomatoes and basil. Whisk again until sauce is hot. Sauce may be kept on a warm stove for a few minutes before serving, but be careful not to let it boil.

Grill swordfish steaks on a slightly oiled, preheated grill, 5 minutes per side. Spoon sauce over steaks and serve.

Serves 4

Tidewater Crabcakes

2 large eggs
1/2 cup finely chopped celery
1 cup crushed saltine crackers
1 tablespoon Dijon mustard
1 teaspoon Old Bay Seasoning
1/2 teaspoon red pepper flakes
2 teaspoons Worcestershire sauce
3 tablespoons chopped parsley
1/2 cup finely chopped scallions
Salt and pepper to taste
1 pound lump crabmeat, with cartilage removed
1/2 cup fresh bread crumbs
2 tablespoons unsalted butter
2 tablespoons vegetable oil

Combine eggs, celery, saltines, mustard, Old Bay Seasoning, pepper flakes, Worcestershire sauce, parsley, scallions, salt and pepper. Blend well. Fold in crabmeat very gently.

Divide the crabmeat mixture into 8-10 equal portions. Shape into flat patties. Dredge patties in bread crumbs and place on foil-covered cookie sheet. Cover and refrigerate for at least 30 minutes before cooking.

Heat the butter and oil in a large, non-stick skillet. Add patties and sauté over medium high heat for 2-3 minutes on each side, or until golden and lightly crisped. Drain on paper towels.

Serves 4-5

Sweet and Spicy Grilled Salmon

1 tablespoon butter
2 shallots, finely chopped
1/4 cup fresh lime juice
1 tablespoon honey
1/8 teaspoon cayenne pepper
1 tablespoon finely chopped ginger
1/4 cup red wine vinegar
2 tablespoons soy sauce
2 tablespoons finely chopped parsley

2 pounds salmon fillets, or four
   1/2-pound pieces

In a small saucepan, sauté shallots in butter until softened. Add the remaining sauce ingredients and stir until well combined.

Prepare the barbecue for medium heat grilling. Baste the salmon liberally with the sauce. Grill the fillets for 7-10 minutes per side depending on their thickness. Baste frequently with the sauce. Remove from the grill and serve immediately, garnished with lime slices and parsley.

Serves 4

Grilled Salmon with Salsa Verde

Salsa Verde
1 cup packed, fresh stemmed parsley,
   preferably Italian
2 large cloves garlic, crushed
2 tablespoons chopped scallions
1/2 cup chopped fresh basil or
   1 teaspoon dried
1 tablespoon anchovy paste
1 large hard cooked egg, chopped
3 tablespoons fresh lemon juice
1/2 teaspoon hot pepper sauce
1/4 teaspoon freshly ground black
   pepper
Salt to taste
1/3 cup plus 2 tablespoons extra virgin
   olive oil

4 salmon steaks, 1-inch thick

In a food processor, combine all the ingredients for the salsa verde except the oil. Slowly add the oil, a little at a time, and process until the sauce thickens. Add remaining oil in a steady stream until it is all well blended and has the consistency of a thick mayonnaise. Let stand to thicken. The sauce can be refrigerated for several hours but should be served at room temperature.

Grill salmon steaks on a slightly oiled, preheated grill, 5 minutes per side. Serve steaks with salsa verde on the side.

Serves 4

Bluefish in Gin

1 1/2 pounds bluefish fillets
4 tablespoons butter, melted
1/3 cup finely chopped onions
2 teaspoons Jane's Crazy Mixed-Up
   Salt
3 ounces of gin or vodka
4 tablespoons butter, melted

Preheat broiler.

Place fillets skin side down in a large shallow pan. Melt 4 tablespoons of butter and pour over the fish. Sprinkle with onions and Salt. Place fish in preheated broiler on middle rack for 5 minutes or until slightly brown.

Add gin to remaining 4 tablespoons of melted butter. Pour over fish and ignite. When the flame has died down, put fish back in broiler on middle rack and cook for an additional 5-10 minutes, depending on the thickness of the fish.

Serves 4

Scallops Florentine

6 tablespoons butter
2 tablespoons minced onion
3 tablespoons minced lettuce
2 tablespoons minced celery
1 teaspoon minced parsley
3 tablespoons dry bread crumbs
1/2 teaspoon anchovy paste
1/4 teaspoon salt
Dash white pepper
36 sea scallops, approximately
   3 pounds
3 tablespoons butter
1 package frozen, chopped spinach,
   thawed and drained

Preheat broiler. Melt 6 tablespoons of butter in a small saucepan over low heat; add all ingredients, except scallops, 3 tablespoons of butter, and spinach. Mix well. Heat with care, and do not let butter brown. Keep warm.

Place scallops on foil lined broiler pan. Dot scallops with 3 tablespoons of butter and broil until lightly browned, about 5 minutes. Divide scallops evenly among 6 small individual baking dishes or shells. Scatter spinach over scallops and drizzle with butter mixture.

Place individual dishes or shells on a baking sheet and place under broiler until heated through.

Serves 6

Do Ahead Coquilles St. Jacques

1/2 cup bread crumbs
1 tablespoon butter, melted
1 1/2 to 2 cups grated Gruyère cheese
1 cup mayonnaise
1/4 cup white wine
1 tablespoon chopped parsley
2 tablespoons butter, melted
1 pound sea scallops
1/2 cup chopped onions
1/2 pound sliced mushrooms

Toss bread crumbs in 1 tablespoon of melted butter and set aside. Mix together Gruyère cheese, mayonnaise, white wine and parsley.

Cook scallops and onions in 2 tablespoons melted butter. When scallops and onions are opaque, remove from heat and drain.

Mix the scallops and onions with the mushrooms and Gruyère mixture. Place all ingredients in a 2-quart casserole and cover with buttered bread crumbs. Recipe may be refrigerated at this point.

Preheat oven to 350 degrees. Cover casserole and bake 20-30 minutes, until bubbly. Remove cover and place casserole under broiler for the last 2 or 3 minutes, until the bread crumbs are nicely browned.

Serves 6

A rich and aromatic blend of scallops, cheese and cream. Complement with the simplicity of Asparagus with Lemon Crumb Topping.

Seafood Elegante

2 tablespoons butter, melted
1 pound mushrooms, sliced
6 tablespoons butter
1/3 cup flour
1 10-ounce can chicken broth
1 1/2 cups heavy cream
1 pound lump crabmeat
1/2 pound medium shrimp, cooked,
   peeled and deveined
3/4 pound bay scallops, poached 2-3
   minutes and drained
1 cup buttered bread crumbs
1 8-ounce package mozzarella cheese,
   shredded
Salt and pepper to taste

Preheat oven to 350 degrees.

Sauté mushrooms in 2 tablespoons melted butter. Drain and set aside. In a medium skillet, melt 6 tablespoons of butter and blend in 1/3 cup of flour. Add chicken broth and cream. Cook until thickened.

Combine crabmeat, shrimp and scallops. In a 3-quart casserole, alternate layers of seafood and mushrooms. Pour sauce over the layers, allowing it to seep to the bottom. Top with buttered bread crumbs. Sprinkle shredded cheese on top and salt and pepper to taste. Bake 30 minutes or until bubbly.

Serves 6-8

Turban of Sole with Shrimp Mousse

8 sole fillets
2 tablespoons fresh lemon juice
2 teaspoons salt
1 teaspoon white pepper

Shrimp Mousse
1 pound raw shrimp
2 egg whites
1 cup heavy cream
1 teaspoon salt
1 tablespoon ketchup
1 tablespoon chopped parsley
2 tablespoons dry sherry
1 tablespoon butter, softened

Sauce
1/4 cup butter
1/4 cup flour
1/2 teaspoon salt
1 cup light cream
1 tablespoon ketchup
2 egg yolks
1/2 cup dry sherry

1/4 pound mushrooms, thickly sliced
Watercress

Rinse sole fillets and pat dry; brush with lemon juice and sprinkle with salt and pepper. Lightly butter a 5-cup ring mold (8½ inches across, 2 inches deep). Line mold with sole fillets, dark side up, narrow end to center, and over-hanging the outside and inside rims.

Mousse: Peel and devein shrimp; wash and pat dry. Place in food processor with egg whites, heavy cream, salt, ketchup, parsley and sherry. Process until smooth. Fill mold with mousse.

Preheat oven to 350 degrees. Fold ends of fillets over top of filling. Spread top with 1 tablespoon soft butter and cover top of mold with a square of waxed paper. To bake, place ring mold in a 14 x 10-inch baking pan. Pour enough boiling water around mold to measure 1 inch. Bake 30 minutes, or just until firm.

Sauce: In a heavy medium saucepan, melt 1/4 cup butter; remove from heat. With wire whisk, blend in flour and salt. Gradually stir in light cream and ketchup. Return to heat. Cook over medium heat, stirring constantly, until mixture comes to a boil and thickens; lower heat and simmer 1 minute. Remove from heat. In a small bowl, beat egg yolks; gradually beat in 1/2 cup of the hot sauce. Stir yolk mixture back into sauce; add sherry. Stir over low heat until hot. Keep warm. Meanwhile, sauté mushrooms in 2 tablespoons butter until tender.

To serve mold, loosen edge of ring; pour off any liquid into sauce. Invert onto heated platter; lift off mold. Spoon sauce over ring. Garnish with watercress and sautéed mushrooms.

Serves 8-10

Layered Snapper and Vegetable Bake

4 tablespoons butter, melted
1/4 pound mushrooms, finely chopped
1 medium carrot, finely chopped
2 scallions, thinly sliced
1 small stalk celery, finely chopped
1/2 cup fresh bread crumbs
1/2 teaspoon dried rosemary
1/2 teaspoon salt
Freshly ground pepper
1½ to 2 pounds red snapper fillets
2 tablespoons butter, melted
2-3 tablespoons dry white wine or chicken broth
Lemon slices for garnish

Preheat oven to 400 degrees. Sauté mushrooms, carrots, scallions and celery in butter until tender, about 5 minutes. Add the bread crumbs, rosemary, salt and pepper.

Rinse the fish fillets and pat dry on paper towels. Butter a baking dish and place half of the fillets in the bottom, skin side down. Cover with the vegetable mixture, then with the rest of the fillets, skin side up. Brush fillets with melted butter. Bake for 30 minutes, basting twice with the remaining butter and wine or broth.

To serve, remove top layer of skin and cut the fish into serving pieces. Remove from the serving dish so that the bottom skin stays in the baking dish. Remove a bit of the vegetable stuffing from the center and place on top of each serving. Garnish with lemon slices.

Serves 4

Marinated Tuna Oriental Style

1/4 cup sherry vinegar
1/4 cup soy sauce
2 teaspoons Dijon mustard
Freshly ground pepper
6 tablespoons sesame oil
6 tablespoons vegetable oil
4 tuna steaks, approximately 1-inch
    thick
Lime slices and coriander sprigs for
    garnish

Combine the vinegar, soy sauce, mustard and pepper in a blender or food processor. With motor running, add the oils in a steady stream and blend until emulsified. Pour marinade over the tuna steaks and let marinate for 2 hours in the refrigerator. Preheat grill.

Grill tuna steaks 4-5 minutes per side, basting frequently with marinade. Garnish with lime slices and coriander.

Serves 4

Delight your guests with an oriental theme. Begin with Chinese Dumplings. Serve the Marinated Tuna as an entrée accompanied by Japanese Cucumber Salad.

Curried Orange Roughy

8 4-ounce orange roughy fillets
1/2 cup mayonnaise
1 tablespoon dry white wine
1 tablespoon lemon juice
1/2 teaspoon dried dill weed
1/2 teaspoon curry powder
Paprika
Minced fresh dill, for garnish

Preheat oven to 350 degrees. Lightly coat a broiling rack with vegetable cooking spray. Place rack in a shallow baking pan; arrange fillets on rack.

Combine mayonnaise, wine, lemon juice, dill and curry powder. Spread over fillets. Bake for 25 minutes or until fish flakes easily when tested with a fork. Sprinkle with paprika and place under a heated broiler for 1-2 minutes. Garnish with minced fresh dill.

Serves 6-8

Grilled Mako with
Roasted Peppers

1 red bell pepper
1 yellow bell pepper

Marinade
3/4 cup plain lowfat yogurt
3/4 cup mayonnaise
1 shallot, minced
2 teaspoons minced fresh tarragon
2 teaspoons minced fresh basil
2 teaspoons fresh lemon thyme
Juice of 1 lemon
3 tablespoons milk

4 6-ounce mako steaks, 1-inch thick

Place peppers in a preheated broiler, turning frequently, until all sides are blackened. Place peppers in a paper bag and seal. When cool, peel and seed peppers. Cut peppers lengthwise into strips. Set aside.

Combine all marinade ingredients. Place mako steaks in a shallow glass baking dish and cover with marinade, turning to coat. Marinate 30 minutes to 1 hour, turning once.

Preheat grill or broiler. Grill or broil steaks 5 minutes; then baste, and cook 5 minutes on the other side, or until cooked through. Place on a serving plate and top with peppers.

Serves 4

Flounder au Gratin

2 tablespoons olive oil
2 pounds fillet of flounder or sole
Onion salt
Freshly ground pepper
1/2 cup mayonnaise
Juice of 1/2 lemon
1/2 cup bread crumbs
1/2 cup chopped parsley
1/2 cup grated sharp Cheddar cheese

Preheat oven to 375 degrees.

Brush large shallow baking dish with olive oil. Sprinkle fish generously on both sides with onion salt and pepper. Place fish in prepared baking dish.

Mix mayonnaise with lemon juice and spread over fish. Sprinkle with bread crumbs. Place in oven for 5 minutes. Remove from oven and sprinkle with parsley and cheese. Place under broiler, about 10 inches from flame until golden brown, approximately 5 minutes.

Serves 6

Stuffed Flounder with Mustard Sauce

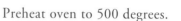

Mustard Sauce
1/2 cup sour cream
1/2 cup mayonnaise
Dijon mustard to taste

3 large scallions, chopped
2 tablespoons oil
1 10-ounce package frozen spinach, thawed, chopped and squeezed dry
4 ounces cream cheese, softened
1 cup cooked rice
1/4 cup chopped walnuts
3/4 teaspoon salt
1/4 teaspoon pepper
1 1/2 teaspoons Dijon mustard
1/4 to 1/2 teaspoon Worcestershire sauce
2 pounds flounder fillets
Salt and pepper
1/2 cup clam juice or fish stock
1/2 cup water

Combine all mustard sauce ingredients and chill.

Preheat oven to 375 degrees. Sauté scallions in oil until soft. Remove from heat and add spinach, cream cheese, rice, nuts, salt, pepper, mustard and Worcestershire sauce. Salt and pepper fillets. Put a tablespoon of filling in the center of each fillet and roll up. Place fillets in a shallow baking dish and add clam juice and water. Cover with wet, wrinkled wax paper. Bake for 12 minutes. Drain and serve hot or chilled, with mustard sauce.

Serves 6

Roasted Monkfish with Ginger and Scallions

6 monkfish fillets, 4 ounces each
6 ounces fresh ginger
3 scallions
2 tablespoons olive oil
1/4 cup peanut oil
1/4 cup sesame oil
1 tablespoon soy sauce

Preheat oven to 500 degrees.

Slice ginger and scallions as thinly as possible and then cut into thin strips; set aside.

Heat olive oil in ovenproof skillet until hot. Cook monkfish in hot oil until browned on both sides, searing in juices. Transfer skillet to the oven and bake fillets for 2 minutes on each side. Meanwhile, combine peanut oil and sesame oil and heat until smoking.

Remove fillets from oven. Top each fillet with strips of ginger and scallions. Splash with soy sauce and ladle a tablespoon of the hot peanut-sesame oil over the fillets to cook the ginger and scallions. Serve immediately.

Serves 6

Contributed by Fountain Restaurant of the Four Seasons Hotel.

The essence of the monkfish blends perfectly with the peanut and sesame oils to delight the senses. Serve with Garlic Snow Peas and close with the White Velvet Tart.

Sumptuous Seafood Strudel

Filling
1/2 pound shrimp, peeled and deveined
1/2 pound scallops
1/2 pound salmon, skin removed
1 10-ounce package frozen spinach,
    thawed and finely chopped
4 tablespoons butter
2 carrots, peeled and sliced
1 onion, peeled and diced
1 clove garlic, minced
1/2 teaspoon salt
1/4 teaspoon pepper
1/2 teaspoon dried sage
1/4 cup dried bread crumbs

Strudel
4 tablespoons butter
12 sheets phyllo dough
1/4 cup dried bread crumbs

Sauce
1/8 cup olive oil
1 tablespoon butter
1 small onion, chopped
1 small carrot, chopped
1 stalk celery, chopped
1 clove garlic, minced
1 15-ounce can tomato sauce
1 tablespoon minced fresh parsley
1 tablespoon minced fresh dill
1/4 teaspoon dried basil
1 tablespoon lemon juice
3 or more drops of hot pepper sauce to
    taste
Salt and pepper

Filling: Cut shrimp and fish into
1-inch pieces. Remove moisture from
spinach. In a large skillet, melt butter
over medium heat and sauté carrots,
onion and garlic until slightly softened.

Add seafood, spinach, salt, pepper and
sage. Cook until seafood turns opaque.
Stir in dried bread crumbs. Set aside.

Strudel: Preheat oven to 400 degrees.
Melt 4 tablespoons butter. Place one
sheet of phyllo dough on a piece of
waxed paper, while keeping remaining
sheets of phyllo moist with a damp tea
towel or paper towels. Brush sheet with
melted butter and sprinkle with dried
bread crumbs. Repeat this process with
5 more phyllo sheets. Spoon half the
seafood filling lengthwise on the phyllo
sheets, covering about one third of the
sheet.

Roll strudel from filling side, tucking
ends under. Repeat this entire process
with the remaining 6 phyllo leaves.
Place both rolls seam side down on an
ungreased cookie sheet and brush with
remaining butter. Bake for 20-25
minutes until golden brown. Cool on
cookie sheet for 5 minutes. Slice on the
diagonal and spoon on strudel sauce.

Sauce: In a saucepan, heat oil and
butter. Add the chopped vegetables and
garlic and simmer over medium heat
for about 10 minutes. Add the tomato
sauce, parsley, dill, basil, lemon juice,
hot pepper sauce, salt and pepper.
Bring to a boil; reduce heat and
simmer, uncovered, for 30 minutes.

Serves 6 as a main course or 12 as a
first course.

Seviche with Tomato Relish

1 pound bay scallops
3/4 cup fresh lime juice

Relish
4 large tomatoes, cored, seeded,
    coarsely chopped and drained
1 red onion, diced
1 12-ounce jar roasted red pepper
    strips, well drained
1/2 6-ounce can pitted black olives,
    drained and coarsely chopped
6 cloves garlic, peeled
1 2-ounce can anchovies
1/2 cup balsamic vinegar
1/4 cup olive oil

Cover scallops with lime juice and
marinate in refrigerator for at least
1 hour. The scallops must be entirely
covered by the juice to "cook".

Combine the tomatoes, onion and
red pepper strips in a large bowl; set
aside. In a food processor or blender,
purée the olives, garlic and anchovies.
Add vinegar and oil and process until
smooth. Add to tomato mixture.

When scallops are ready, drain well
and add to relish. Chill and serve.

Serves 6 as a main course, 12 as a first
course

Poultry

Roast Chicken Stuffed with Mushrooms

1 6-7 pound roasting chicken
1 large clove garlic, cut in half
Salt and pepper
1 pound mushrooms, cut into quarters
2 sprigs fresh thyme, chopped or
   3/4 teaspoon dried
1/2 cup chopped parsley
2 cups whole pearl onions (optional)

Preheat oven to 425 degrees. Oil a roasting rack and place it in a roasting pan which has been filled with 1/4 inch of water.

Rub outside of chicken and inside the cavity with the garlic. Sprinkle the chicken inside and out with salt and pepper. Toss the mushrooms in a large bowl with the thyme and parsley. Stuff the chicken with the seasoned mushrooms, reserving the excess mushrooms. Truss the chicken.

Roast chicken about 1¼ hours to 1¾ hours, lowering the heat to 375 degrees after 1/2 hour. Baste every 30 minutes. After 1 hour, stir the remaining mushrooms and pearl onions into the bottom of the roasting pan. Remove from oven when juices run clear when chicken is pricked. Let stand 10 minutes before cutting. Use mushrooms as garnish.

Serves 4-6

Winter's Roasted Chicken

8 tablespoons butter, softened
8 chicken breast halves
12-15 new potatoes, scrubbed but not
   peeled
12 shallots, peeled
8 sprigs of fresh thyme
Salt and pepper to taste
1 tablespoon flour
1 cup chicken broth

Preheat oven to 400 degrees. Butter a roasting pan large enough to hold the chicken in one layer.

Rub breasts with remaining butter and place skin side up in pan. Cut potatoes and shallots in half. Scatter potatoes, shallots and thyme around chicken. Sprinkle with salt and pepper. Cover pan and roast for 15 minutes. Uncover pan, baste and continue roasting until potatoes are done, about 25-30 minutes.

Transfer chicken, shallots, and potatoes to a platter and keep warm. Pour 2-3 tablespoons of the drippings into a small saucepan, heat, and add flour. Cook, whisking until golden. Add chicken broth and continue stirring until sauce is smooth. Simmer over low heat for about 5 minutes, adjust salt and pepper to taste. Drizzle sauce over chicken.

Serves 6-8

A cozy winter supper of heavenly aromas when served with Carrot Purée and ended with warm Simply Pecan Pie.

Chutney Baked Cornish Hens

4 Cornish hens, split in half and
   trimmed of excess fat
3 tablespoons butter, softened
Salt and pepper to taste
6 tablespoons vinegar
2 cloves garlic
1 cup vegetable oil
1 cup chutney

Preheat oven to 300 degrees.

Wash hens and pat dry. Rub with soft butter. Season with salt and pepper. Put hens in a broiler pan, skin side down.

Combine vinegar, garlic, oil, and chutney in a food processor and process until smooth. Broil hens for 4-5 minutes on one side, basting with chutney sauce and drippings. Turn over and repeat for 4-5 minutes on other side. Put hens into baking pan and cover with remaining chutney sauce. Bake for 25-35 minutes, basting as necessary.

This recipe is also good grilled outdoors. In this case, bake first, then finish on the grill. Use less sauce, as it will burn. Instead, pass extra chutney.

Serves 8

Chicken Livers in Wine

1/2 cup butter
1/4 cup finely chopped onion
1/4 cup finely chopped parsley
2 pounds chicken livers, cut apart if connected
2 teaspoons dried tarragon
2 teaspoons salt (optional)
Dash pepper
1/4 cup white wine

In a large skillet, sauté onion and parsley in butter until onion is softened. Add the chicken livers and sauté, stirring frequently, until cooked throughout. Livers will be done when they are barely springy to the touch, about 5-7 minutes; do not overcook. Transfer livers to a warm platter. Stir tarragon, salt, pepper, and wine into pan juices; bring to a boil. Remove from heat. Pour the cooked livers into the sauce and stir to coat. Serve on a bed of rice.

Serves 6-8

Honey Nut Drums

4 tablespoons butter
1/4 cup honey
2 tablespoons Dijon mustard
16 chicken drumsticks
3/4 cup bread crumbs
3/4 cup finely chopped pecans
Salt and pepper to taste

Preheat oven to 350 degrees.

Melt butter over medium heat. Stir in honey and mustard and simmer for 5-8 minutes. Remove from heat. Using pastry brush, brush legs all over with the butter mixture. Combine bread crumbs, pecans, salt and pepper in medium bowl. Roll drumsticks in the breadcrumb mixture, then place on a cookie sheet. Bake until tender and brown, 30-45 minutes.

Yields 16 drumsticks

Turkey Marsala

1 pound turkey cutlets
2 tablespoons flour
3 tablespoons extra virgin olive oil
3 tablespoons butter
1 clove garlic, cut in half
Salt and pepper to taste
3 tablespoons lemon juice
3/4 cup Marsala wine
1/2 cup mushrooms, thinly sliced
6-8 thin slices mozzarella cheese (optional)
3 tablespoons chopped parsley
1 lemon, cut into thin slices

Dredge turkey cutlets in flour. In a skillet, heat the oil and butter until hot. Add the garlic halves. Quickly brown turkey on both sides. Lower heat, sprinkle with salt and pepper, add lemon juice, Marsala wine and mushrooms. Simmer 4-5 minutes. Remove garlic. If desired, top turkey with the mozzarella slices for the last minute. Garnish with parsley and lemon slices.

Serves 4

Marsala is a light, sweet, white wine that brings a distinct and delicious flavor to the mushroom sauce.

Spicy Garlic Sesame Stir Fry

1/2 teaspoon pepper
2 tablespoons soy sauce
3 tablespoons chicken broth
1 tablespoon sugar
2¼ teaspoons lemon juice
1/4 teaspoon crushed red pepper flakes
    (more if you prefer very spicy)
3 tablespoons sesame oil
2 large cloves garlic, minced
1 teaspoon cornstarch mixed with
    1½ teaspoons water
2 tablespoons sesame oil
1/2 pound boneless, skinless chicken
    breasts, sliced into 1/2-inch strips
1¼ cups broccoli florets
1/2 cup mushrooms, thinly sliced
Salt to taste

Combine the pepper, soy sauce, chicken broth, sugar, lemon juice, and crushed red peppers in a small bowl and set aside. In a small saucepan, heat the 3 tablespoons sesame oil over medium to high heat, being careful not to burn the oil. Sauté the garlic until it turns yellow, but not brown. Add the soy sauce mixture and bring to a boil. Whisk in the cornstarch mixture, turning the heat off as soon as the sauce starts to thicken.

Heat 2 tablespoons sesame oil in a wok or heavy skillet on high heat. Add chicken and stir fry about 2 minutes, until the chicken turns white. Stir in broccoli, mushrooms and sauce and stir fry until broccoli turns bright green and is slightly tender, about 4 minutes. Season with salt, to taste. Serve over steamed rice.

Serves 2

Moroccan Chicken

3 large onions, sliced
1 tablespoon vegetable oil
2 tablespoons flour
5 pounds chicken pieces, skin removed
1½ teaspoons salt
1/2 teaspoon pepper
16 ounces pitted prunes
1/2 cup yellow currants (optional)
2 cups tomato sauce

Preheat oven to 350 degrees.

Place sliced onions in a 4-quart casserole. Drizzle with oil and sprinkle with flour. Arrange half of the chicken on top. Season with half the salt and pepper and scatter with half of the prunes and currants. Pour half the tomato sauce over all. Repeat layers with remaining ingredients. Cover and bake 2 hours until chicken is tender.

Serves 8

A robust combination of flavors complemented by the color and texture of Saffron Rice.

Kung Pao Chicken with Peanuts

1 pound boneless, skinless chicken
    thighs, cut into 1/2 inch cubes
1/2 teaspoon salt
2 eggs
3 tablespoons cornstarch
2 tablespoons soybean or sunflower oil
2 cups soybean or sunflower oil
1/3 cup diced bamboo shoots
1/3 cup diced celery
1/3 cup diced water chestnuts
1½ teaspoons Oriental chili paste
1 teaspoon chopped scallions, white
    part only
1 cup chicken broth
3 tablespoons soy sauce
1 teaspoon sugar
1 teaspoon dry sherry
3/4 cup snow peas
1/4 cup julienne red pepper
3 tablespoons cornstarch
1 teaspoon sesame oil
1 cup unsalted roasted peanuts

Blend salt, eggs, cornstarch and 2
tablespoons oil. Marinate chicken in
mixture for at least 20 minutes.

Put 2 cups oil in a wok and heat. Stir
fry chicken in oil until light gold in
color. Add bamboo shoots, celery and
water chestnuts for 30 seconds. Remove
chicken and vegetables with a strainer
and set aside. Discard oil in wok,
except for 3 tablespoons. Reheat wok
with 3 tablespoons of reserved oil.
When oil is hot, stir fry chili paste and
scallions for 30 seconds.

Mix chicken broth, soy sauce, sugar,
and sherry, add to wok. When liquid
boils, add chicken and all vegetables,
including snow peas and red pepper, to
wok. Mix well. Remove 1/4 cup of
liquid from wok and blend with 3
tablespoons of cornstarch. Add to wok
and stir quickly. Add sesame oil and
peanuts and stir fry briefly. Serve over
steamed white rice.

Serve 4-6

*Bright in color and pungent in flavor,
this stir fry promises to be a treat for
the palate. Finish with the cool and light
Sweetheart Creams.*

Commonwealth Curried Chicken

2 tablespoons butter
1½-2 pounds boneless, skinless chicken
    breasts, cut into 1-inch cubes
3 tablespoons butter
1 cup chopped onion
1 cup chopped, unpeeled tart apple
    (such as Granny Smith)
1 clove garlic, crushed
5-6 teaspoons curry powder
1/4 cup flour
1 teaspoon salt
1/4 teaspoon ground ginger
1/4 teaspoon ground cardamom
1/4 teaspoon pepper
3½ cups chicken broth

In a medium saucepan, sauté the
chicken in 2 tablespoons of butter until
the chicken has turned completely
white. Remove the chicken.

In the same saucepan, sauté onion,
apple, garlic, and curry in 3 tablespoons of butter over medium high
heat for about 5 minutes. Remove
from heat. Stir in flour, salt, ginger,
cardamom, and pepper. Gradually stir
in broth. Bring to a boil, stirring constantly. Return chicken to the saucepan. Simmer uncovered 20 minutes,
stirring occasionally.

Serve over steamed white rice. When
entertaining, pass the following
condiments in separate bowls: chopped
onion, chopped green pepper, raisins,
coconut, chutney, peanuts and chopped
mandarin oranges.

Serves 6

Chicken Dijon in Phyllo

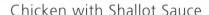

Chicken with Shallot Sauce

Sauce
1½ cups mayonnaise
1 cup chopped scallions
1/3 cup lemon juice
3 cloves garlic, minced
2 teaspoons fresh dill
1 tablespoon Dijon mustard

12 boneless, skinless chicken breast
    halves
Salt and pepper
24 sheets phyllo dough
1⅓ cups butter, melted
2/3 cup freshly grated Parmesan cheese

Combine first 6 ingredients to make a sauce. Lightly sprinkle chicken pieces with salt and pepper. Place a sheet of phyllo on working surface. Quickly brush with melted butter. Place a second sheet on top of the first. Brush with melted butter. Spread about 1½ tablespoons of sauce on each side of a chicken breast. Place breast in one corner of buttered phyllo sheets. Fold corner over breast, then fold sides over and roll breasts up in the sheets to form a package. Place in an ungreased baking dish. Repeat with remaining breasts and phyllo sheets. To prevent the phyllo dough from drying out, keep it covered with plastic wrap and a damp cloth, removing only one sheet of dough at a time.

Brush packets with the rest of the butter and sprinkle with Parmesan cheese. At this point, the dish may be tightly sealed and frozen. Thaw completely before baking.

Bake at 375 degrees for 20-25 minutes, or until golden. Serve hot.

For a quick alternative, instead of preparing the mayonnaise dill sauce, spread each chicken breast with 2 tablespoons of Boursin cheese and 1 teaspoon finely chopped scallions before rolling in phyllo dough.

Serves 12

Creamy Dijon chicken is hidden beneath delicate layers of buttery phyllo leaves and dusted with freshly grated Parmesan cheese for a lovely do-ahead entrée.

4 boneless, skinless chicken breast
    halves
Salt and pepper to taste
3 tablespoons butter, divided
1/4 cup finely chopped shallots
3 sprigs fresh thyme
1 tablespoon balsamic vinegar
1/3 cup dry white wine
1½ teaspoons Worcestershire sauce
1/2 cup chicken broth
2 teaspoons tomato paste
1/3 cup heavy cream
1½ tablespoons Dijon mustard
Parsley to garnish

Sprinkle breasts with salt and pepper to taste. Melt 2 tablespoons butter over medium high heat in a sauté pan. Add chicken breasts and brown lightly on each side. Remove to a platter and keep warm.

Add the remaining tablespoon of butter, the shallots, and thyme. Cook until the shallots are softened. Add vinegar, wine and Worcestershire sauce and deglaze. Add the broth and return to a boil. Add the tomato paste. Reduce liquid by half, lower heat, then add the cream and mustard.

To serve, spoon sauce over chicken breasts and garnish with parsley.

Serves 4

Apricot Chicken

3/4 cup dried apricots
2 cups water
8 boneless, skinless chicken breast
  halves
3 tablespoons flour
1 tablespoon curry powder
2 teaspoons salt
4 tablespoons vegetable oil
1 small onion, chopped
2 tablespoons brown sugar
2 chicken bouillon cubes
1 cup water
1 teaspoon lemon juice
2 tablespoons soy sauce
1 8¾-ounce can apricot halves (packed
  in water, if available)

Preheat oven to 350 degrees.

Place dried apricots and 2 cups water in
a small saucepan. Bring to a boil, then
simmer uncovered for 12 minutes.
Remove from heat and cool slightly.
Place cooked apricots and liquid in a
food processor and purée. Set aside.

Completely coat chicken breasts in a
mixture of the flour, curry powder and
salt, and brown very lightly in oil in a
frying pan. Remove chicken and place
in a large baking dish.

Sauté onion in frying pan drippings
until translucent. Stir in brown sugar,
bouillon, water, lemon juice, soy sauce
and apricot purée. Heat to boiling,
then pour over chicken. Bake, covered,
for 1/2 hour, or until chicken is tender.
For the last 5 minutes of baking, top
each piece of chicken with an apricot
half and glaze with pan drippings. Dish
should remain covered for the last 5
minutes.

Serves 6-8

*A beautiful presentation with Sesame
Green Beans tied in bundles and molded
mounds of Perfect Rice Every Thyme.*

Breast of Chicken with Raspberry Vinegar

4 boneless, skinless chicken breast
  halves
Salt and pepper to taste
1 tablespoon butter
1½ teaspoons minced fresh tarragon or
  1 teaspoon dried tarragon
1 shallot, minced
1 clove garlic, minced
1/3 cup dry white wine
1½ teaspoons raspberry vinegar
1 plum tomato, seeded and coarsely
  chopped
1/3 cup heavy cream

Place the chicken breasts between
sheets of waxed paper and pound to
an even thickness. Season to taste with
salt and pepper. Sauté the chicken in
butter, turning to brown both sides.
Add tarragon, shallot, garlic and wine.
Cover and simmer 15 minutes. Transfer the chicken to a heated serving dish
and keep warm. Add vinegar to pan
juices and reduce by one half over medium high heat. Scrape the pan to deglaze it. Add chopped tomato and heat
through. Pour in the cream and reduce
to form a slightly thickened sauce.
Spoon over chicken and serve immediately. If preparing ahead, do not add
the cream until immediately prior to
serving. The finished sauce will separate if kept over heat for any length of
time.

Serves 4

Chicken Duxelles

Filling
8 tablespoons butter
6 tablespoons minced shallots
1 pound mushrooms, finely chopped
4 tablespoons flour
Salt and pepper to taste
2 pinches dry mustard
Fresh lemon juice to taste
1 cup light cream

Chicken
8 boneless, skinless chicken breast
   halves
1 tablespoon brandy
Salt and pepper to taste
2 tablespoons butter
2 tablespoons oil
2 tablespoons warmed brandy
2 tablespoons minced shallots
1 small clove garlic, minced
1 teaspoon dried tarragon
1/4 cup white wine
1 1/2 cups chicken broth
1 1/2 tablespoons cornstarch mixed with
   2 tablespoons water

Heat 8 tablespoons butter in a heavy
skillet over high heat. Add shallots and
mushrooms and sauté, stirring until all
moisture has evaporated. Add flour,
salt, pepper, mustard and a few drops
of lemon juice. Add cream and simmer
until thickened. Correct seasonings.

Cut a slit in each chicken breast to
form a pocket. Brush pocket with
brandy and add 1-2 teaspoons of the
mushroom filling. (You will use about
one half of the mushroom filling to fill
8 pieces of chicken.) Press the pocket
closed and sprinkle chicken with salt
and pepper. In a heavy skillet, brown
the chicken (pocket side down) in
2 tablespoons each of oil and butter,
using a heavy weight, such as a lid, to
hold it flat. Turn and brown other side.
When nicely browned, remove from
pan. Remove pan from heat. Deglaze
pan with 2 tablespoons warmed
brandy. Return pan to heat, add
shallots and garlic and cook 1 minute
without browning. Add tarragon, wine
and broth. Bring to a boil and return
chicken to pan. Cover and simmer
until tender, about 20 minutes. Use the
cornstarch and water mixture to
thicken sauce as desired.

Warm the remaining mushroom
mixture. To serve, top each piece of
chicken with 1-2 teaspoons of the
mixture.

Serves 8

Bahamian Chicken

6 chicken breast halves
2 tablespoons butter
Salt and pepper to taste
1 1/2 cups orange juice
1/2 cup raisins
1/2 cup chutney
1/2 cup chopped almonds
1/2 teaspoon curry
Dash of thyme

Preheat oven to 425 degrees.

Place breasts skin side up in a buttered
shallow casserole dish. Rub each breast
lightly with butter and season with salt
and pepper to taste. Bake for 15
minutes. Reduce oven temperature to
350 degrees.

Combine orange juice, raisins, chutney,
almonds, curry and thyme in a small
saucepan and simmer gently for 10
minutes, stirring frequently. Pour sauce
over chicken and continue baking
chicken for 30-45 minutes, until juices
run clear when chicken is pricked.

Serves 6

Chicken Dijon Supreme

3/4 cup flour, seasoned with 1 teaspoon
   each of salt and pepper
4 boneless, skinless chicken breast
   halves
1/4 cup butter
1/4 cup olive oil
2 teaspoons minced shallots
1/2 cup dry vermouth
2 tablespoons brandy
6 teaspoons Dijon mustard
1/4 teaspoon salt
1/4 teaspoon coarsely ground pepper
1 cup heavy cream
3-4 teaspoons minced parsley

Preheat oven to 200 degrees.

Coat chicken in seasoned flour. Heat
butter and oil in a skillet and sauté
breasts over medium high heat for 5
minutes on each side. Remove chicken
from skillet and keep warm in oven.

Drain oil and butter from skillet,
retaining any brown bits. Add shallots,
vermouth and brandy, turn heat to
high, and reduce the amount of liquid
to approximately 4 tablespoons. Whisk
in mustard, salt, pepper and cream and
cook over medium heat for 2-3
minutes, stirring until the mixture is a
smooth sauce. Place each chicken breast
on a plate and top with sauce and
parsley.

Serves 4

Chicken and Yogurt

6 boneless, skinless chicken breast
   halves
Salt and pepper to taste
4 tablespoons butter
2 tablespoons olive oil
1/2 cup chopped onion
1/2 pound mushrooms, sliced
1 cup plain yogurt
Juice of 1 lemon
1 tablespoon fresh, chopped basil
1 tablespoon flour
4 tablespoons sliced almonds, lightly
   toasted

Season chicken with salt and pepper to
taste. In 2 tablespoons butter and 1
tablespoon olive oil, sauté chicken until
lightly browned. Remove the chicken
and keep warm.

Add the remaining butter and oil to the
pan. Add onion and cook until it is
opaque. Add the mushrooms and
continue cooking until the liquid from
the mushrooms begins to evaporate.
Whisk in yogurt, lemon juice, basil and
flour, and stir until the sauce is
smooth. Return chicken to pan and
simmer until the chicken is tender. Top
with toasted almonds.

Serves 6

Chicken Camarillo

6 boneless, skinless chicken breast
   halves
2 tablespoons butter
2 ripe avocados, peeled and sliced
2 teaspoons grated ginger
1/2 cup chicken broth
1/2 cup heavy cream
1/4 cup butter
1 small onion, finely chopped
1/4 cup crumbled, cooked bacon

Preheat oven to 400 degrees.

In a skillet, sauté the chicken breasts in
2 tablespoons of butter for about 10
minutes. Remove from heat.

In a food processor, process avocados,
ginger, chicken broth and cream until
smooth. Sauté onion in butter until
golden, then add to avocado mixture.

Place cooked chicken breasts in a
lightly greased, oblong baking dish.
Pour the avocado mixture over the
chicken. Sprinkle with the crumbled
bacon. Bake until bubbly, about 20
minutes.

Serves 6

Sunshine Chicken

4 chicken breast halves
1 6 ounce can frozen orange juice
   concentrate
1/2 cup brown sugar
3 tablespoons lemon juice
1 tablespoon soy sauce
1/2 teaspoon garlic powder
1/2 teaspoon paprika
Dash of nutmeg (optional)
1 teaspoon shredded orange peel

Preheat oven to 325 degrees.

Place chicken, skin side up, in a baking dish. Mix orange juice, brown sugar, lemon juice, soy sauce, garlic powder, paprika and nutmeg together and pour over chicken. Bake for 1 hour, basting every 20 minutes. Top each breast with 1/4 teaspoon shredded orange peel for the last 5 minutes of baking.

Serves 4

Mexican Chicken

1 cup medium hot chunky taco sauce
1/2 cup Dijon mustard
4 tablespoons fresh lime juice
6 boneless, skinless chicken breast
   halves
2 tablespoons butter
6 tablespoons plain yogurt
1 lime, peeled, sliced into 6 segments
6 teaspoons coarsely chopped fresh
   cilantro

In a large bowl, mix taco sauce, mustard and lime juice. Add chicken, turning to coat. Marinate for at least 30-45 minutes.

In a large skillet, melt butter over medium heat until foamy. Remove chicken from marinade and place in skillet. Cook about 20 minutes, turning to brown both sides. Add marinade and cook 5-10 minutes longer, or until fork can be inserted into chicken with ease. Remove chicken to a platter. Raise heat to high and boil marinade for at least 1 minute.

To serve, pour sauce over chicken. Place 1 tablespoon yogurt on each breast half and top each with a lime segment and 1 teaspoon of cilantro.

Serves 6

Begin the fare with Seviche with Tomato Relish. Gather a fiesta of colors with this flavorful chicken, Jalapeño Cornbread and a salad of greens dressed with Lime Ginger Dressing.

Santa Fe Chicken

4 boneless skinless chicken breast
   halves
4 pieces Monterey Jack cheese, about
   1/4 inch thick and 1½ x 3-inches
   long
1 3-ounce can chopped green chilies
2 eggs
1 teaspoon grated Parmesan cheese
1/4 teaspoon salt
1/4 teaspoon pepper
1 tablespoon minced fresh parsley
3/4 cup flour
1/4 cup butter or oil
4 sprigs fresh parsley

Preheat oven to 375 degrees. Cut a 2-inch deep pocket in the side of each chicken piece, being careful not to cut through. Place strip of cheese and a teaspoon of green chilies in each pocket. Chill.

In a large bowl, beat together eggs, Parmesan cheese, salt, pepper and parsley. Roll breasts in flour; dip into egg mixture.

Heat butter or oil in skillet. Sauté breasts just until crisp and golden, turning with a spatula. Breasts may be refrigerated at this point and finished just before serving.

Transfer chicken to a buttered baking dish and bake for 8-10 minutes, or until coating begins to brown. Garnish with parsley.

Serves 4

Meat

Savory Beef Brisket

3 to 4½ pound beef brisket
1 cup barbecue sauce
1/2 cup water
1/2 cup chopped onion
1/4 cup Liquid Smoke
1/4 cup Worcestershire sauce
1 tablespoon garlic powder
2 teaspoons celery salt
2 teaspoons lemon pepper
1 teaspoon salt
2 beef bouillon cubes

Preheat oven to 300 degrees.

Mix all ingredients except beef brisket in a dutch oven. Turn brisket in mixture to coat thoroughly. Place fat side up and bake uncovered for 5-6 hours.

Before serving, pull brisket apart with fork. Serve on Cracked Pepper Sandwich Rolls.

Serves 8-10

Cajun Beef

3 to 4-pound eye of round roast
1/4 cup instant minced onion
1/4 teaspoon instant minced garlic
1 tablespoon salt
1½ teaspoons ground black pepper
3/4 teaspoon red pepper
3 tablespoons water
1/4 cup cider vinegar

Preheat oven to 350 degrees.

Score 1½-inch deep slits along top and sides of beef. Mix together the onion, garlic, salt, black pepper, red pepper, water and vinegar. Using a spoon, open slits wide enough to insert some of the mixture into each slit. Continue until all slits are filled. If any mixture remains, pour over top of beef. Marinate beef overnight.

Transfer beef to a medium sized roasting pan, pouring all liquid over beef. Wrap beef loosely in foil wrap and cook approximately 1¼ hours for medium rare.

Serves 6-8

Grilled Skewered Beef

1½ pounds beef tenderloin, cut into
    1½ inch cubes
3 tablespoons olive oil
4 tablespoons butter, melted
2 tablespoons fresh thyme or
    1 teaspoon dried
1½ tablespoons Dijon mustard
1/8 teaspoon red pepper flakes
4 tablespoons butter, melted
Salt and pepper
6 tablespoons lemon juice

Preheat barbecue grill.

Divide the beef among 4 barbecue skewers. Combine oil, 4 tablespoons melted butter, thyme, mustard, and red pepper flakes. Mix well. Brush over all sides of the beef cubes. Season to taste with salt and pepper. Grill 3 minutes per side, brushing with the oil mixture.

Combine remaining 4 tablespoons melted butter with lemon juice. Heat quickly and pour over the meat just before serving.

Serves 4

Welcome summer by multiplying this recipe and gathering your friends for the season's first barbecue. Offer big baskets of herbed butter breadsticks and a platter of Summer Greens. A perfect close is the decadent Chocolate Mousse Pie.

Balsamic Marinated
Rib-Eye Steaks

4 rib-eye steaks, about 1½ inches thick
4 shallots, finely chopped
2 large cloves garlic, minced
1/2 cup balsamic vinegar
1/2 cup soy sauce
2 tablespoons olive oil
Pepper

Preheat barbecue grill.

Combine shallots, garlic, vinegar, soy sauce and olive oil in a non-metallic bowl. Mix thoroughly. Pepper the rib-eye steaks to taste and place them in a 9 x 13-inch non-metallic dish. Pour marinade over steaks and lift steaks so that marinade is on top and bottom of the steaks. Cover with plastic wrap and marinate in the refrigerator overnight. Grill 5 inches over hot coals for 4 minutes. Turn and grill for 3 minutes more for medium rare.

Serves 4

Marinated Flank Steak

1 to 2-pound flank steak
3/4 cup vegetable oil
1/4 cup soy sauce
2 teaspoons red wine vinegar
1/2 teaspoon ground ginger
2 large cloves garlic, minced
6 scallions, chopped
3 tablespoons honey

Preheat barbecue grill.

Combine marinade ingredients. Place flank steak in marinade and turn to coat thoroughly. Marinate for up to 2 days, turning occasionally.

Grill over hot coals, 5-7 minutes per side for medium rare. Slice against the grain.

Serves 4-6

Italian Stir Fry

1½ pounds mild Italian sausage, cut into sections
1 pound fresh green beans, cut into 1-inch sections
1 large red onion, sliced
1 red pepper, chopped
2 cloves garlic, minced
1/4 cup red wine vinegar
1/2 teaspoon oregano
1/2 teaspoon basil

In large skillet or wok, brown and cook sausage until done, approximately 15 minutes. Cut sections further into approximately 1-inch pieces. Remove to a plate and keep warm.

Add green beans to drippings and stir fry until crisp-tender. Add onion, pepper, and garlic to green beans and continue to stir fry approximately 5 minutes until peppers are crisp-tender. Return the sausage to the pan and add the vinegar, oregano and basil and stir fry 5 minutes over high heat.

Serves 4-6

Minted Grilled Lamb Chops

4 large lamb chops (or 8 small)
1/2 cup dry white wine
1/4 cup chopped fresh mint leaves
Salt and pepper
1 shallot, chopped
1/3 cup minced fresh mint leaves
1/3 cup dry white wine
1/4 cup lemon juice
2 tablespoons water
3 egg yolks
1/4 pound unsalted butter, softened
4 mint sprigs

Trim lamb chops of excess fat. Combine 1/2 cup white wine and 1/4 cup chopped mint leaves. Pour marinade over the chops and marinate while preparing the grill and ingredients for sauce.

Remove chops from marinade and salt and pepper to taste. Grill over medium high coals 4-5 minutes per side for medium rare. Meanwhile, in a small saucepan, combine chopped shallot, 1/3 cup mint leaves, 1/3 cup white wine, lemon juice and water. Reduce over moderate heat until almost all of the liquid has evaporated. Whisk the reduction into the egg yolks in top of double boiler. Place over barely simmering water and continue to beat until mixture has become thick and fluffy. Turn off the heat and whisk in butter a little at a time until sauce is smooth and thickened. To serve, spoon sauce over lamb chops and garnish with the mint sprigs.

Serves 4

Lamb with a Twist

1/2 cup juniper berries
1 1/2 cups gin
1 leg of lamb, boned
Salt and pepper
2 lemons
1/2 cup gin (optional)

Soak juniper berries in gin overnight in an airtight container.

Flatten out leg of lamb, season cut side with salt and pepper to taste and spread the juniper berries over the seasoned lamb. Grate peel of 1 lemon and spread over lamb. Squeeze juice of the lemon over the lamb. Roll up lamb and marinate in juice of second lemon and the 1 1/2 cups gin.

Approximately 1 hour before serving, place lamb on a roasting rack or rotisserie and cook at 425 degrees for approximately 45 minutes for medium rare. Baste with juices while cooking. Let stand 10 minutes before carving. Flame first with 1/2 cup gin, if desired. Serve with pan juices.

Serves 8

An irresistible combination of flavors! Add to the intrigue with Asparagus Soufflé and a finale of Crème Brûlée.

Butterflied Lamb Beaujolais

1 cup Beaujolais
Juice and grated peel of 1 orange
2 cloves garlic, minced
1/4 cup fresh thyme
1/4 cup light olive oil
1/2 teaspoon salt
1 leg of lamb, butterflied

Make marinade by combining all ingredients in a small bowl. Place the leg of lamb in a large, shallow, airtight container and pour the marinade over, making sure it is evenly distributed. Refrigerate for at least 6 hours, preferably overnight.

Remove from marinade. Grill over hot coals to sear meat for about 3 minutes on each side. Cover and grill each side for about 20-25 more minutes for medium rare. Place the lamb on a wooden carving platter and let rest for about 10 minutes. Slice against the grain and serve garnished with a sprig of fresh thyme.

Serves 8

Brandied Pork Chops

6 boneless pork chops, 3/4 to 1-inch
    thick
6 tablespoons unsalted butter
Salt and pepper
1/2 pound Gruyère or Swiss cheese,
    finely grated
3 tablespoons Dijon mustard
3 tablespoons heavy cream
6 tablespoons Applejack brandy
5 tablespoons heavy cream
2 tablespoons minced fresh parsley

Preheat oven to 350 degrees.

Melt butter in a 12-inch ovenproof
skillet over moderate heat. Brown
chops approximately 5 minutes per
side. Season chops with the salt and
pepper to taste. Cover skillet and bake
in oven for approximately 40 minutes
or until just done.

Mix together cheese, mustard, and 3
tablespoons heavy cream. When chops
are done, remove from oven and spread
with the cheese mixture.

Broil chops 3-5 inches from flame until
the tops are brown and bubbly.
Remove chops to serving platter and
keep warm.

Add Applejack brandy to pan and stir
over medium high heat, scraping up
browned bits. Add remaining 5
tablespoons heavy cream and simmer,
stirring until sauce is slightly
thickened.

Pour sauce over chops and sprinkle
with parsley.

Serves 4 to 6

Fall Pork

8 center cut boneless pork chops
2 tablespoons butter
2 cloves garlic, minced
1 cup white wine
Salt and pepper
2 tablespoons chopped fresh oregano
2 tablespoons butter
8 Granny Smith apples, peeled, cored,
    and thinly sliced
1/3 cup firmly packed brown sugar
2/3 cup heavy cream
8 scallions for garnish

Arrange pork chops in a 9 x 13-inch
non-metallic baking dish. Heat butter
in a medium skillet and sauté the garlic. Add wine, salt and pepper. Remove
from heat and add the oregano. Pour
marinade over the pork and marinate
overnight in the refrigerator.

Drain the meat, reserving the
marinade. Strain the marinade into a
small saucepan and boil over medium
high heat approximately 5 minutes or
until slightly syrupy. Heat the
remaining 2 tablespoons butter in a
large, deep skillet and sauté apple slices
until soft, approximately 10 minutes.
While apples cook, grill pork over
medium hot coals 3-4 minutes per side
or until done. When apples are sautéed,
add brown sugar, cream, and reduced
marinade. Cook until sugar is
dissolved.

To serve, distribute sauce among 4
plates. Arrange 2 chops on top of each
serving and garnish with scallions.

Serves 4

Gingersnap Roast Pork

2½-3 pound boneless pork loin roast
1/4 cup butter
1/3 cup finely chopped onion
1/3 cup finely chopped green pepper
1/4 cup finely chopped celery
2 large cloves garlic, minced
1 teaspoon salt
1/2 teaspoon pepper
1/2 teaspoon paprika
1 teaspoon dried thyme
1/2 teaspoon dry mustard

Gingersnap Gravy
2 tablespoons butter
1/2 cup finely chopped onion
1/4 cup finely chopped celery
1 garlic clove, minced
1/2 teaspoon ground ginger
1/4 teaspoon salt
1/8 teaspoon pepper
1/4 teaspoon dried thyme
1/8 teaspoon dried sage
Dash cumin
8-10 ginger snap cookies, crushed

Preheat oven to 325 degrees. Place roast in a shallow roasting pan, fat side up. Score 1½-inch deep slits in top and sides of roast.

Melt butter in a medium skillet and sauté onion, green pepper, celery, garlic, salt, pepper, paprika, thyme and mustard until the vegetables are softened. Using a spoon, stuff the vegetable mixture into the slits in the pork roast.

Roast pork until internal temperature reaches 170 degrees, approximately 2 hours. Remove roast from pan and keep warm.

Gravy: Add enough water to pan drippings to make 2 cups total liquid. Using the liquid, deglaze the pan over medium high heat for approximately 2 minutes, scraping up the browned bits from the pan bottom. Remove from heat.

In a medium sized skillet, melt 2 tablespoons butter and sauté onion, celery, and garlic until vegetables are tender. Add the ginger, salt, pepper, thyme, sage, and cumin and sauté for an additional 2 minutes. Add the ginger snap cookies and stir until moistened. Add the pan juice liquid to the skillet and stir until blended and thickened.

To serve, pour some of the gravy over the roast. Pass remaining gravy separately.

Serves 4-6

Gingersnaps are the hidden ingredient in the rich and robust gravy. As the roast bakes, the aromas enchant!

Scotched Ham

1 8-10 pound ham
3 tablespoons Dijon mustard
Whole cloves
1½ cups Scotch or Bourbon
1½ cups dark brown sugar

Preheat oven to 350 degrees. Score ham into 1-inch squares and brush with mustard. Place a clove at each intersection of score.

Heat liquor and add sugar. Stir until dissolved and continue cooking until the glaze has thickened slightly. Brush mixture over ham.

Bake ham in a roasting pan for approximately 15 minutes per pound, brushing with the glaze about four more times during the last 45 minutes. Any remaining glaze may be served with the ham. If desired, the amount of the glaze may be doubled, and the ham may be sliced and served in the glaze.

Serves 10-12

Veal with Fresh Corn

1¼ pounds veal cutlets
Salt and pepper
3 ears of corn (approximately 1 cup
   kernels)
1 tablespoon sugar
1/4 cup white vinegar
1/4 cup flour
1½ tablespoons oil
2 tablespoons butter
3 tablespoons finely chopped shallots
1/3 cup dry white wine
1/2 cup chicken broth
1/4 cup heavy cream
2 teaspoons Dijon mustard

Preheat oven to 200 degrees. Pound veal lightly with a flat mallet. Sprinkle both sides with salt and pepper to taste. Cut kernels from cobs of corn. In a non-metallic bowl combine corn, sugar and vinegar. Set aside until ready to use, stirring occasionally.

Coat veal with flour and shake off excess. Heat oil and butter in a 10-inch sauté pan. Add veal and sauté for 2-3 minutes on each side. Remove from pan and keep warm in preheated oven. Add shallots to pan and cook briefly. Add wine and deglaze the pan. Drain corn, discarding liquid. Add corn and chicken broth and bring to a boil, reducing liquid for 5 minutes. Add cream and mustard and cook 2 minutes until hot. Pour sauce over veal.

Serves 4-6

Veal Tarragon

1 pound veal cutlets
Pepper
1/4 cup flour
3 tablespoons butter
1 large clove garlic, minced
2/3 cup cognac
2/3 cup chicken broth
2 tablespoons chopped fresh tarragon
1/2 cup heavy cream
1 teaspoon cornstarch

Preheat oven to 200 degrees. Pound veal lightly and cut into serving pieces. Sprinkle fresh ground pepper on both sides of veal and dredge in flour.

In a 10-inch sauté pan, melt the butter. Add garlic and sauté for 1 minute. Add veal and sauté until lightly browned, approximately 2-3 minutes on each side. Transfer veal to plate and place in warm oven.

Add cognac to the pan and bring to a boil. Add chicken broth and tarragon and reduce the mixture by one-third over medium high heat. Reduce heat to medium low. Add cream and simmer for 5 minutes. Dissolve cornstarch in a small amount of water and add to sauce, stirring constantly until thickened. Stir in any liquid from veal plate.

Arrange veal on serving platter and pour sauce over veal.

Serves 4

Lemony Veal

1½ pounds veal loin, cut into 8 pieces
3 tablespoons flour
1½ tablespoons oil
3 tablespoons vermouth
Juice of 1½ lemons (slightly less than
   1/3 cup)
1½ teaspoons fresh chopped chives
1½ teaspoons dried chervil
1 cup chicken broth
1/2 teaspoon butter

Preheat oven to 200 degrees. Dredge veal in flour, tapping to remove excess. Heat oil in a 10-inch skillet and brown veal 1-2 minutes on each side. Remove veal and keep warm in the oven. Deglaze the pan with the vermouth and add the lemon juice, chives, chervil, and broth. Bring to a boil, reducing by one-third. Return veal to pan and simmer 1 minute. Stir in butter. Serve immediately.

Serves 4-6

Garnish with thin slices of lemon and single strands of fresh chives for a light and lovely entrée.

Veal Byrds

10 large veal cutlets
1 8-ounce package seasoned bread
    crumb stuffing mix
8 bread slices, crusts removed and cut
    into small cubes
2 stalks celery, minced
1 small onion, minced
3 tablespoons minced fresh parsley
1/2 teaspoon poultry seasoning
1 teaspoon salt
1/2 teaspoon pepper
1 tablespoon fresh rosemary or 1/2
    teaspoon dried
1 tablespoon fresh thyme or 1/2
    teaspoon dried
4 tablespoons butter, melted
3/4 cup beef broth

4 tablespoons butter, melted
4 tablespoons oil

1 cup red wine
1¾ cups beef broth
1/2 pound mushrooms, sliced
3 tablespoons cornstarch
Salt and pepper

Preheat oven to 200 degrees. Pound
veal until 1/4-inch thick and season
with salt and pepper. In a large bowl,
combine stuffing mix, cubed bread,
celery, onion, parsley, and spices. Add
4 tablespoons of melted butter and
blend. Add 3/4 cup beef broth to lightly
moisten stuffing. Place approximately
1/4 cup stuffing in center of each veal
cutlet. Roll the cutlets and secure with
toothpicks.

In a 12-inch skillet, combine remaining
4 tablespoons butter with 4 tablespoons
oil and heat over medium high heat.
Add rolled veal and sauté until
browned on all sides, approximately 5-
10 minutes. Remove and keep warm in
heated oven.

To skillet, add red wine and remaining
beef broth, stir and bring to a boil.
Reduce heat. Add mushrooms and
simmer 5 minutes. Dissolve cornstarch
in a small amount of water; gradually
stir into sauce to thicken. Add salt and
pepper to taste. Return veal to skillet
and heat through.

Serves 6-8

*So elegant and yet so easy. Simply prepare
the veal rolls in the morning and sauté
them just before serving.*

Winter Veal Stew

1 cup flour
1 tablespoon paprika
1 tablespoon garlic powder
1 tablespoon ground pepper
2 pounds veal, cut into 1 inch cubes
1-2 tablespoons shortening
3 large yellow onions, sliced into
    1/4-inch slices
3 cups white wine
3 cups water
6 chicken bouillon cubes
12 red potatoes, unpeeled, halved
12 carrots, sliced into 1/2-inch slices
1 large white onion, finely chopped
1 12-ounce bag frozen peas
1 pint heavy cream

Combine flour, paprika, garlic powder
and pepper in a paper bag. Drop in veal
pieces one handful at a time and shake
to coat with flour mixture. Remove
from bag and set aside.

Heat shortening in a stew pot and
when hot, add veal pieces and brown.
Remove meat from pot. Add yellow
onions to the pot, sauté until limp.
Return meat to the pot and add the
wine, water and bouillon cubes. Cook
over moderate heat for 1/2 hour. Add
potatoes, carrots, and white onion and
cook another 1/2 hour or until potatoes
and carrots are cooked through. The
stew can be refrigerated or frozen at
this point. Before serving, add peas and
cream. Heat until piping hot
throughout.

Serves 6-8

Table and Wine Presentations

Imagine yourself as an artist and the table a blank canvas. Before composing your work of art, visualize the moment. Select the location for its intimacy or grandeur. Will the gathering be familiar or just getting acquainted? Is the occasion festive or sublime, frivolous or elegant? Is the table round, oblong or square?

Once you have set the mood, think about how you will create your effects. Consider the lighting – candles or a crackling fire? And now the table top; simplicity here can be dramatic. Tuck a bundle of fresh basil in a handwoven basket or a mountain of lemons and limes in a white porcelain bowl. Scatter lightly oiled walnuts and apples among twisted ivy. Tie ribbons around the stems of your wine glasses or fashion napkin rings out of brightly colored shoelaces. Place a fresh gladiola at each place or tie a sachet in the folds of the ladies' napkins. Hide a framed baby picture of the birthday celebrant among the gifts. Spread a rag rug or a patchwork quilt on your table. Tie a wide ribbon around the neck of a wooden duck and let its long tails intertwine the baskets of food. Pour orange juice in stemmed crystal glasses. Begin a collection of hand-painted eggs or brass candlesticks or antique tea cups and let your collection tell a story. Whatever you do and however you do it, savor the opportunity to express yourself.

Every sense is keen when we come together for a meal. Startle the senses with enticing aromas. Add an element of surprise with sparkling crystal against tapestry linens, colorful foods on white plates, or stirring music against a quiet night. Calm the senses with aromas from childhood, delicate china, a spray of pastels and Mozart. You are limited only by your imagination and spontaneity.

In this hurried world, coming together for a meal is a welcome respite from the demands of work and play. A thoughtful setting offers an opportunity to relax, to reflect, to be refreshed. Bring this gift to your table.

In determining which few words we might share about wine presentation, all of our wine consultants stressed the sport of experimentation.

Though adept in the kitchen, many a host and hostess feel less confident about pairing wine with food. The goal, however, is simply to enhance the character of each. To make a great match, consider the predominant characteristics of the wine and food: tastes (fruity, meaty, lemony, earthy), textures (heavy, light, rich, silky) and physical components (acidity to balance fats, tannin to balance protein). Pairing is usually complementary (such as light wine with light food, sweet wine with desserts), but can be provocative if contrasting.

"Classic" matches include young Chianti with a pasta and seafood dish, Sauvignon Blanc with flounder, and Burgundy with lamb. Presenting a contrast that works well takes more knowledge (or a wine retailer's advice) about the highlights of each wine and the food. To experiment, try a young Rhone with swordfish or a Barolo with our Lemony Veal. The fruit and texture of these wines contrasts with the food, for a sum greater than the parts.

Often, you will discover that the perfect match can be complementary and contrasting on different levels. One example is Stilton cheese and Sauterne. Their tastes contrast (pungent versus fruity), their textures are complementary (rich in both cases), and their physical components contrast (saltiness versus sweetness).

Regionalism – pairing local foods and wines – offers its own rewards. Almost every region of the country has some wonderful wines that naturally go well with foods produced there. Serve a tangy, fresh, Lancaster County goat's-milk cheese with crisp, fresh Pennsylvania Seyval Blanc. Or try a mid-Atlantic (Pennsylvania, Maryland, Virginia) Chardonnay with our Tidewater Crabcakes.

But in the end, remember that wine is just one component of the special setting you create. Follow the experts' advice and experiment!

Among William Penn's most treasured legacies are the many open spaces he dedicated as city parks or "squares." Today, from sunrise to starlight, Philadelphia's Fairmount Park is teeming with joggers, cyclists, rowers, sports enthusiasts, picnickers, music lovers and tourists by the trolley-full. With 8,500 acres of grand diversity, it is the largest landscaped city park in the world. Within, you will find several restored, late 18th-century "country estate" mansions, the Japanese Tea House, outdoor concert pavilions, museums, tennis courts, a golf course, playing fields and the Philadelphia Zoological Gardens.

Beyond the city limits, one can easily visualize Revolutionary soldiers coming over the rolling hills at Valley Forge National Park or the Brandywine Battlefields. The beauty of Longwood Gardens offers a feast for the senses.

For spectators, the city is sports heaven. From sculling and regattas on the Schuylkill River to the annual Penn Relays Carnival – one of the nation's most prestigious track and field events – to the CoreStates Bike Race, Philadelphia leads the pack in amateur sporting events. Professionally, the city is known for its loyal and vocal enthusiasm for the Phillies in baseball, the Eagles during football season, the Flyers in hockey, and the 76'ers basketball team.

Finally, we would be remiss not to mention the fine equestrian events which exist throughout the Delaware Valley. From steeplechases and hunts to the Devon Horse Show and Country Fair, equestrians will raise one's awareness of the status Philadelphians place on play.

*The polar bears live in
Bear Country at the
Philadelphia Zoological
Gardens which opened its
doors in 1874.*

*Indoor and outdoor
year-round botanical
displays can be
seen at Longwood Gardens,
once the country home of
Pierre du Pont.*

*Swann Memorial Fountain
by Alexander Stirling
Calder sits at the center
of Logan Circle, designated
by Penn as one
of America's first parks.*

*Fairmount Park's
four-acre Azalea Gardens,
a gift from the Pennsylvania
Horticultural Society
in 1952, is enjoyed by all.*

*Penn's Landing
on the Delaware River
is where Penn first
glimpsed his 47,000 square
mile "sylvania."*

*Built in the 1850's,
the nine Victorian turreted
boathouses, referred
to as Boathouse Row, are
headquarters to nine
Philadelphia rowing clubs.*

Fairmount Park's Japanese
House and Garden, called
Shofu-So, is a replica
of an early 17th century
country estate.

The 175 acres of formal
gardens and woodlands of
Morris Arboretum
are a haven for outstanding
specimen trees.

Blessed with both bayside
and oceanside views,
Cape May, New Jersey
opens its classic Victorian
homes to visitors
from around the world.

Vegetables

Summer's Delight

6 ears fresh corn, preferably Silver
   Queen
2 teaspoons sugar
1/2 cup butter
3/4 teaspoon freshly ground pepper
2/3 cup heavy cream
1/2 teaspoon salt

Cut corn from cob. Combine corn with sugar; chill 1 hour.

Melt butter in saucepan over medium heat. Add corn and cook for 4 minutes. Stir in pepper. Gradually add cream, stirring constantly. Cook, uncovered, over medium heat 12-15 minutes until liquid is absorbed. Stir in salt.

Serves 6-8

The memory of this summer treat will linger long after summer is gone.

Asparagus with
Lemon Crumb Topping

1/4 cup butter
1/2 cup chopped cashews
1 cup bread crumbs
1 lemon
1 tablespoon grated lemon zest
1/2 cup minced parsley
1 to 2 pounds asparagus
Lemon slices for garnish

In a skillet over medium heat, melt butter. Add cashews and sauté for 3 minutes. Add bread crumbs and continue to sauté until browned, about 5 minutes. Cut 1 lemon in half and squeeze juice into bread crumb mixture. Stir in lemon zest and parsley.

Steam asparagus until just tender. Arrange on a serving platter and sprinkle with crumb topping. Garnish with lemon slices. Serve immediately.

Serves 8

Sesame Green Beans

4 teaspoons soy sauce
1 teaspoon sugar
1 teaspoon sherry
1 tablespoon sesame seeds
1½ tablespoons vegetable oil
3 cloves garlic, minced
1 tablespoon minced fresh ginger
1 pound fresh green beans, ends
   trimmed, cut on diagonal

In a small non-metallic bowl, stir together soy sauce, sugar and sherry; set aside.

Heat wok or heavy skillet and cook sesame seeds, stirring constantly, until lightly browned, 3-5 minutes. Remove and set aside. Increase heat and pour in oil. Stir in garlic, ginger and beans. Cook, stirring for 1½ minutes. Stir in soy sauce mixture. Cover wok, reduce heat to medium and cook beans until tender and crisp, about 7 minutes. Uncover, increase heat to high and bring to a boil, stirring frequently until liquid has almost evaporated, 1-3 minutes. Pour beans into serving dish and sprinkle with sesame seeds.

Serves 4-6

Summer Beans

1/3 cup extra virgin olive oil
2 cups finely chopped red onion
4 large cloves garlic, minced
4 tablespoons fresh mint or 2
    tablespoons dried
1 28-ounce can plum tomatoes,
    chopped, drained
Salt and pepper to taste
2 pounds whole wax beans

In a large skillet, sauté onion in oil
until soft. Add garlic and mint and
cook for 2 minutes. Stir in tomatoes,
salt and pepper; simmer for 15
minutes, stirring occasionally. Add wax
beans and cover; simmer for 30
minutes, stirring occasionally, until
beans are very tender.

Hint: Flavor improves if made 1-3 days
in advance.

Serves 8

Carrots with Apricots

6 tablespoons butter
1 medium onion, cut in thin strips
1½ pounds carrots, cut in thin strips
3 ounces dried apricots, cut in thin
    strips
1/2 teaspoon sherry vinegar
1/2 cup chicken stock, or more as
    needed
Salt and pepper to taste

Heat butter in a large skillet or wok
over medium to high heat. Add onions
and cook until lightly colored. Add
carrots and apricots to pan and sear.
Stir fry for 4 minutes. Add sherry
vinegar and chicken stock. Cover and
cook 5 minutes. Uncover and boil off
most of the liquid. Season to taste with
salt and pepper. The carrots may be
prepared 1-2 days ahead and gently
reheated before serving.

Serves 6

Brussels Sprouts with Caraway

1 pound brussels sprouts
3 tablespoons butter
1 small yellow onion, minced
1 teaspoon caraway seeds
1/4 teaspoon paprika

Trim stem end of sprouts and cut in
half lengthwise through the core. Steam
9-12 minutes, depending on size, until
sprouts are nearly cooked as desired.
Melt half the butter in a large skillet.
Add minced onion and caraway seeds
and sauté for about 5 minutes until
clear. Add remaining butter. Add
sprouts and sauté to brown slightly.
Sprinkle with paprika and stir to mix.

Serves 4

Broccoli with Garlic

2 tablespoons olive oil
3-4 large cloves garlic, minced
2 cups fresh broccoli florets
3/4 cup chicken bouillon
1/4 cup white wine
1/2 lemon

Heat olive oil in 10 inch skillet and sauté minced garlic until lightly browned. Place broccoli in skillet and mix well. Pour bouillon and wine over broccoli and stir. Cover and simmer for 5 minutes until desired tenderness. Pour juice of 1/2 lemon over broccoli and serve.

Serves 4

Broccoli with Blue Cheese

3 cups fresh broccoli florets
2 tablespoons butter
2 tablespoons flour
1 cup milk
1 3-ounce package cream cheese
1/4 cup blue cheese, crumbled
1/2 cup fresh cracker crumbs
1 tablespoon butter, melted

Preheat oven to 350 degrees.

Steam broccoli until tender. Set aside. In a medium skillet over medium heat, melt butter. Stir in flour. Gradually add milk, whisking constantly. Add cream cheese and crumbled blue cheese. Stir in broccoli. Pour mixture into a lightly buttered 2-quart casserole. Top with cracker crumbs. Drizzle with melted butter and bake for 35 minutes.

Serves 6

Zucchini Grate

2 pounds small zucchini
1 tablespoon coarse salt
3 tablespoons butter
1 large or 2 small shallots, chopped
Fresh ground pepper to taste

Wash zucchini and remove ends; grate. Put grated zucchini in colander and add salt. Toss gently and allow to stand for 10 minutes. Rinse zucchini and squeeze dry. Melt butter in a medium skillet. Add chopped shallots and sauté until softened. Add zucchini and sauté 3-4 minutes. Serve immediately.

Serves 4

Colorful Cauliflower

1 head cauliflower (approximately
    2 pounds)
2 cups dry white wine
6 tablespoons olive or corn oil
5 tablespoons fresh lemon juice
2 cloves finely chopped garlic
1/2 teaspoon pepper

Dressing
1/2 pound fresh spinach
2 tablespoons capers
2 tablespoons chopped parsley
2 tablespoons chopped watercress
2 tablespoons chopped black olives
2 tablespoons chopped pimento
Pinch cayenne pepper

Preheat oven to 400 degrees.

Carefully cut off stem and partially
core the cauliflower, making sure to
keep the head intact. Soak cauliflower
in cold water for 30 minutes; drain and
place in baking dish stem side down.
Mix white wine, oil, lemon juice, garlic
and pepper well. Pour mixture over
cauliflower. Cover and bake until
tender, approximately 40-45 minutes.

Dressing: While cauliflower is cooking,
wash and dry spinach and place in the
refrigerator. Combine remaining
dressing ingredients and chill.

To serve, place chilled spinach on a
round platter surrounding the centered
head of cauliflower. Pour any
remaining juices from the baking dish
over the cauliflower. Take the chilled
dressing and sprinkle it over the
spinach and cauliflower. Serve
immediately.

Serves 6-8

*A spectacular presentation with an
equally spectacular taste.*

Garlic Snow Peas

1½ tablespoons peanut oil
2 large cloves garlic, minced
1 pound fresh snow peas, cleaned and
    strings removed
1 teaspoon sesame oil
Salt to taste
Sesame seeds

Add peanut oil to wok or skillet. Stir
fry garlic until lightly browned (be
careful not to burn); set aside. Add
snow peas and stir fry until tender but
crispy. Add browned garlic to wok.
Remove to serving dish and mix with
sesame oil and salt. Sprinkle sesame
seeds on top.

Serves 4-6

Asparagus Soufflé

3 tablespoons butter
4 tablespoons flour
1 1/2 cups milk
6 egg yolks, room temperature
1 tablespoon chopped chives
1 tablespoon fresh parsley
5 tablespoons grated Parmesan cheese
1 cup cooked asparagus, cut into small
    pieces (tough ends omitted)
1/8 teaspoon salt
1/8 teaspoon cream of tartar
8 egg whites, room temperature

Butter a 6-cup soufflé dish. Extend top of dish about 2 inches by attaching a strip of greased paper around the dish. Remove strip before serving.

Melt the butter until foamy, then stir in the flour until mixture is pasty. Whisk in the milk slowly for a smooth, thick sauce. Remove the pan from the heat, and continuing to whisk, add the egg yolks, one at a time. (This basic soufflé sauce can be prepared a day in advance. Refrigerate in a tightly closed container and reheat slightly before proceeding.)

Preheat oven to 350 degrees. Add the seasonings, cheese, and pieces of asparagus to the soufflé sauce. In a bowl, add salt and cream of tartar to the egg whites and beat them until they are stiff but still smooth and moist. (If beating egg whites in an unlined copper bowl, cream of tartar may be omitted).

Lightly mix about a cupful of the beaten egg whites into the sauce, then gently fold in the rest until barely mixed. Spoon carefully into the prepared soufflé dish and gently place it in the center of the oven. Bake 35-40 minutes or until it has risen high above the dish and does not wobble when tapped.

Serves 6

Spectacular in its presentation, this soufflé can be partially prepared ahead and finished just before serving.

Winter Greens

3 to 5 cloves garlic
2-3 teaspoons sesame oil
1/2 to 1 teaspoon hot chili oil
1 tablespoon lemon juice
1 teaspoon soy sauce
2 teaspoons fresh ginger, peeled,
    minced
1 10-ounce package frozen greens
    (spinach, kale, collard, turnip or
    mustard greens)
1 tablespoon sesame seeds

Press garlic cloves through a garlic press. Mix together garlic, oils, lemon juice, soy sauce and minced ginger. Set aside. Cook the greens according to package directions. When just thawed, stir in garlic mixture and finish cooking, being careful not to overcook or brown. Sprinkle with sesame seeds and serve in a radicchio leaf or in a grilled sweet red pepper half.

Hint: Larger amounts of ingredients should be used with greens other than spinach.

Serves 4

Baked Tomatoes

6-8 firm tomatoes, uniform in size if
    possible
1/4 cup butter
1/2 cup lemon juice
1/2 cup light brown sugar
1½ teaspoons cinnamon
1 tablespoon grated onion
1 bay leaf
1½ teaspoons rosemary
Pinch sweet basil
Pinch garlic powder

Preheat oven to 350 degrees.

Dip tomatoes in boiling water to remove skin. Place in a large baking dish.
In a saucepan, mix the remaining
ingredients and cook for about 10 minutes or until mixture is syrupy. Pour
mixture over the tomatoes in the baking dish. Bake for 45 minutes to 1hour.
Baste frequently so that tops of tomatoes do not dry out. Depending on the
number of tomatoes used, you may
wish to reserve half of the sauce and
freeze for another time.

Serves 6-8

Eggplant Tomato Bake

1 large eggplant (1¾ pounds)
2 teaspoons salt

2 eggs, beaten
2 tablespoons butter, melted
2 teaspoons salt
1/4 teaspoon pepper
1/2 teaspoon oregano
1/2 teaspoon basil
1/4 teaspoon garlic powder or 1 clove
    garlic, minced
1/2 cup dry bread crumbs
1 small onion, chopped
4 ounces Cheddar cheese, grated
2 large ripe tomatoes, sliced
1/4 cup grated Parmesan cheese
Paprika

Preheat oven to 350 degrees.

Peel and slice eggplant. Cover and cook
in salted water for 10 minutes. Drain
and mash. Stir in eggs, butter, salt,
pepper, oregano, basil, garlic, bread
crumbs, onion and 1/2 of the Cheddar
cheese.

Grease a 2-quart casserole and arrange
1/2 of the tomato slices on the bottom.
Add the eggplant mixture and top with
remaining tomato slices. Sprinkle
evenly with remaining Cheddar cheese
and Parmesan cheese. Dust with
paprika. Bake for 1 hour.

Serves 6-8

Saffron Rice

1/4 cup minced onion
2 tablespoons olive oil
1 cup rice
1/4 teaspoon crushed saffron
1/4 teaspoon salt (optional)
2 tablespoons currants
2 cups chicken broth
1/4 cup fresh chopped parsley
1/4 cup toasted pine nuts

In a medium saucepan, sauté onions
in olive oil until soft and yellow. Add
rice and saffron. Cook, stirring, for 1
minute. Add salt, currants and broth.
Bring to a boil, cover; reduce heat and
simmer 20 minutes or until moisture is
absorbed. Add parsley and toasted pine
nuts; stir.

Serves 4-6

Untamed Rice

2 ounces dried porcini or wild
mushrooms
3/4 cup unsalted butter
3 tablespoons olive oil
2 bunches scallions, chopped
2 carrots, peeled and finely chopped
1/2 cup chopped pecans
1 cup egg noodles, uncooked
2 cups long grain rice
4 cloves garlic, minced
1 pound fresh mushrooms, sliced
1 cup minced fresh parsley
1/2 cup dry white wine
4-5 cups beef or chicken broth
Salt and pepper to taste
2 cups freshly grated Romano or
   Parmesan cheese
2 eggs
1½ cups heavy cream

In a small bowl, put dried mushrooms in hot water and cover. Let stand 30 minutes.

Melt 4 tablespoons butter and 1 tablespoon olive oil in a large skillet over medium heat. Add scallions, carrots and nuts. Sauté for 10 minutes until lightly browned. Remove from heat to a large bowl.

Melt 4 tablespoons butter and 1 tablespoon olive oil in same skillet; add egg noodles and rice. Stir to coat and brown for 10 minutes. Remove from heat; set aside.

Melt 4 tablespoons butter and 1 tablespoon olive oil in same skillet; add

garlic and sauté until lightly browned. Add drained mushrooms (reserve liquid), fresh mushrooms and parsley. Sauté 15 minutes uncovered. Season with salt and freshly ground pepper.

Transfer all ingredients into a large pot and add reserved mushroom liquid, white wine and enough broth to completely cover the rice mixture. Cover and simmer over low heat for 20-30 minutes, adding more broth if necessary. Be careful to cook until tender and firm only.

Preheat oven to 350 degrees. Butter a 2-quart baking dish. Spread 1/2 the rice mixture on the bottom of the dish. Top with 1 cup of the cheese. Spread remaining rice mixture on the top.

In separate bowl, whisk eggs and cream together and pour evenly over rice casserole. Top with remaining cheese. Bake for 30 minutes or until golden brown and puffed. Serve immediately.

Serves 12

A wild and exotic coming together of many tastes and textures, well worth the effort.

Perfect Rice Every Thyme

1½ tablespoons butter
1/4 cup finely chopped onion
1 cup rice
1½ cups chicken broth
1 bay leaf
1/4 teaspoon dried thyme
1/2 tablespoon chopped fresh parsley
Fresh parsley sprig

Preheat oven to 400 degrees.

Melt butter in ovenproof baking dish with lid. Add onion and sauté until translucent. Add rice and cook until grains are opaque and slightly browned. Pour in chicken broth. Season with bay leaf, thyme and parsley. Stir and bring to a boil. Remove from heat, cover and put in oven. Bake for exactly 17 minutes. Remove from oven, toss and garnish with sprig of fresh parsley.

Hint: This dish may be cooked entirely on top of the stove by reducing heat after reaching a boil, and simmering, covered, for 17 minutes.

Serves 4

Sweet Potato Carrot Purée

2 large sweet potatoes, approximately 2
    to 2½ pounds
3-4 large carrots, approximately
    1 pound
1/2 cup water
1/2 cup unsalted butter, softened
1 cup sour cream
1 teaspoon freshly grated nutmeg

Preheat oven to 375 degrees.

Scrub potatoes and cut small slit in
each. Bake for approximately 1 hour or
until tender.

Peel carrots and cut into 2-inch slices,
then cut slices in half. Place in a
saucepan with water and bring water to
a boil. Cook covered until water has
almost evaporated, about 30 minutes.
Drain off any excess water.

Peel sweet potatoes and combine with
carrots in a food processor or blender.
Add butter, sour cream and nutmeg.
Process until smooth. Place in a 2-quart
casserole dish, cover and bake at 325
degrees for 25 minutes.

Serves 8

Carrot Purée

2 to 2¼ pounds carrots, peeled, cut
    into 1-inch pieces
1/2 cup milk
2 large eggs
1/2 teaspoon vanilla
1 teaspoon Dijon mustard
1/4 teaspoon freshly ground pepper
3 tablespoons unsalted butter

Preheat oven to 350 degrees.

Add peeled, cut carrots to a saucepan of
boiling water. Return water to a boil
and boil for 20-25 minutes or until
carrots are quite tender; drain.

In a food processor, purée carrots until
smooth. Add milk. eggs, vanilla,
mustard, pepper and 2 tablespoons of
unsalted butter. Purée until smooth.

Pour mixture into a well buttered
1-quart casserole dish. Dot with
remaining 1 tablespoon unsalted
butter. Bake, uncovered, for 45
minutes. The casserole may be prepared a day ahead and refrigerated
overnight before baking.

Hints: Lowfat milk may be used and
the last tablespoon of butter eliminated
for the fat-conscious gourmet.

For entertaining, the casserole is
attractive if baked in a ring mold and
served surrounded with baby spring
peas.

Serves 6-8

Carrot Potato Medley

8 carrots, peeled and sliced
2 medium potatoes, peeled and sliced
1 egg
2 tablespoons sour cream
2 tablespoons chopped onion
1/2 teaspoon salt
1/4 teaspoon pepper
2 ounces Cheddar cheese, grated
1 tablespoon butter
Halved orange slices for garnish

Preheat oven to 350 degrees.

Cook carrots in boiling water for 10
minutes. Add potatoes and cook 15
minutes longer. Drain and mash to
desired consistency. Add remaining
ingredients and stir until well blended.
Place in a lightly buttered 1½-quart
casserole. Dot with butter. Bake for 30
minutes. Place under broiler for 3
minutes to brown top. Garnish with
orange slices and serve.

Serves 6-8

Perfect Potato Pie

1 10-inch unbaked pie shell
1 pound cottage cheese
2 cups unseasoned mashed potatoes
    (instant mashed potatoes may be
    used)
1/2 cup sour cream
2 eggs
2 teaspoons salt
1/2 teaspoon cayenne pepper
1/2 cup thinly sliced scallions
3 tablespoons grated Parmesan cheese

Preheat oven to 425 degrees.

Put cottage cheese through sieve or
food mill to make smooth. Beat
mashed potatoes into cottage cheese.
Beat in sour cream, eggs, salt and
cayenne pepper. Stir in scallions. Spoon
into pastry shell. Sprinkle top with
grated cheese. Bake for 50 minutes or
until golden brown.

Serves 8

Potatoes and Celeriac au Gratin

4 Idaho potatoes, (1½ pounds)
1 celeriac (3/4 pound)
2 tablespoons lemon juice
1 tablespoon olive oil
1/4 teaspoon minced garlic
4 ripe tomatoes, (1 pound), peeled, cut
    into 1/2-inch cubes
Salt and freshly ground pepper to taste
6 fresh basil leaves
3/4 cup heavy or light cream
1/4 teaspoon freshly grated nutmeg
1/4 pound grated Gruyère cheese

Rinse potatoes and put into saucepan
with cold water to cover and salt to
taste. Bring to boil and simmer 15
minutes. Drain, and when cool enough
to handle, peel and cut into 1/2-inch
slices.

Peel the celeriac and cut into 1/4-inch
slices and put into a saucepan with
water to cover. Add lemon juice and a
little salt. Bring to a boil and simmer
10 minutes. Drain, reserving 1/2 cup of
the cooking liquid.

Preheat oven to 375 degrees.

Heat oil in skillet. Add garlic,
tomatoes, salt, pepper and basil leaves.
Cook, stirring, for 1 minute. Add
cream, the 1/2 cup of reserved cooking
liquid and nutmeg. Bring to a boil and
simmer 2 minutes.

Grease an oval au gratin dish
(2½ x 8 x 10) with butter. Arrange
potatoes in one layer. Sprinkle with 1/2
of the cheese. Place the celeriac slices
on top. Pour the tomato mixture on
top and sprinkle with the remaining
cheese. Place in the middle of the preheated oven and bake for 40 minutes
until nicely browned.

Serves 4

Barley Bravo

1 cup pearl barley
1 medium onion, chopped
1/2 cup butter
1/2 cup slivered almonds
1/2 teaspoon salt
1¾ cups chicken broth
1/2 cup beef broth
3 teaspoons dried onion
1½ cups fresh mushrooms, sliced
1 8-ounce can water chestnuts, drained, sliced

Preheat oven to 350 degrees.

In a medium skillet, sauté barley and onion in butter until softened. Add all other ingredients and stir to mix. Pour into well buttered 9 x 13-inch pan. Bake, uncovered, until liquid is absorbed, about 1 hour.

Serves 8

The crunchy and nutty quality of this dish offers a unique respite from potatoes and rice.

Baked Butternut

1 average butternut squash, at least 2 cups cubed
4 tablespoons butter
1/4 cup diced onion
2/3 cup grated mild Cheddar or Monterey Jack cheese
1/2 cup mayonnaise
2 eggs, beaten
Salt and pepper to taste
Bread crumbs or wheat germ

Preheat oven to 350 degrees.

Peel squash. Slice in half lengthwise and remove seeds and pulp. Cut into 1-inch cubes. Steam squash until soft, 10-15 minutes. Mash squash in a medium bowl. Combine other ingredients with squash. Pour into a greased 2-quart baking dish. Top with bread crumbs or wheat germ. Bake for 30-40 minutes.

Serves 8

Glazed Sweet Potatoes

5 medium sweet potatoes, peeled
3 tablespoons cornstarch
2 cups orange juice
1 cup brown sugar
1/4 cup raisins
1/2 teaspoon grated orange zest
1/2 teaspoon salt
1/3 cup butter
1/3 cup sherry
1/3 cup pecans, chopped

Preheat oven to 325 degrees.

Parboil potatoes 10-15 minutes; drain and cool. Slice into 1/2-inch pieces and arrange in a lightly buttered 9 x 13-inch baking dish.

Blend cornstarch into 1/4 cup of the orange juice. In a small saucepan, heat remaining orange juice, brown sugar, raisins, orange zest and salt. Add cornstarch mixture and cook over high heat until thickened, about 5 minutes. Stir in butter, sherry and pecan pieces. Pour over potatoes. Bake for 30 minutes, basting occasionally.

Serves 8-10

Mushrooms Diane

12 ounces fresh mushrooms
2 tablespoons butter
3/4 cup sour cream
1 tablespoon Worcestershire sauce
1 teaspoon prepared mustard
1/2 teaspoon dried thyme
Freshly ground pepper

Clean and trim mushrooms. Cut into a similar size, either slicing or halving, depending on the size of the mushroom. In a skillet, melt butter and sauté mushrooms over medium heat, stirring frequently, until cooked through and almost all of the liquid has evaporated. Add other ingredients, stir and cook until blended into a sauce and heated through, about 3-4 minutes. Cook longer to reduce sauce, if necessary. Season with pepper to taste.

Can be served in puff pastry shells, but if so, do not reduce sauce too much.

Serves 2

Mushrooms in Cream Sauce

1 pound fresh mushrooms, cleaned, stems removed
3 tablespoons butter, softened
1 tablespoon minced fresh parsley
1 tablespoon minced onion
1 tablespoon Dijon mustard
1 teaspoon salt
1/8 teaspoon cayenne pepper
1/8 teaspoon nutmeg
1 1/2 tablespoons flour
1/2 to 1 cup heavy cream

Preheat oven to 375 degrees.

Place mushrooms in a lightly buttered 1-quart casserole; set aside. Cream together butter, parsley, onion, mustard, salt, cayenne pepper, nutmeg and flour. Dot this mixture over the mushrooms. Pour cream over all. Cover and bake for 1 hour. Stir twice while baking.

Hint: Serve on your buffet table as an accompaniment to Standing Rib Roast.

Serves 6

Sweet and Saucy

6 tablespoons butter
6 tablespoons brown sugar
2 teaspoons Dijon mustard
2 teaspoons horseradish
1 1/2 teaspoons salt
Dash pepper

Melt butter in medium saucepan. Add brown sugar and dissolve. Add mustard, horseradish, salt and pepper; cook over low heat until warm. Pour over cooked green beans, peas, carrots or cauliflower.

Yields 3/4 cup

Add a spark to a freshly steamed vegetable with the piquant taste of this marvelous sauce.

Brunch

Spinach and Cheese Custard

1 loaf French bread, day old preferred
1 large onion, chopped
2 tablespoons butter
8 cups fresh spinach leaves, cooked and
    chopped
1 teaspoon dill weed
1 teaspoon salt
Freshly ground pepper
1½ cups shredded Swiss cheese
3 large eggs
2½ cups milk
1/4 teaspoon hot pepper sauce

Cut bread into thin slices. Line bottom
of a buttered, shallow 6-cup oblong
baking dish with half the slices.

Sauté onion in butter in large skillet for
5 minutes. Squeeze spinach dry and
add to pan with dill, 1/4 teaspoon salt
and 1/4 teaspoon pepper. Stir just to
combine.

Spread spinach over bread in pan;
sprinkle with 1 cup of cheese. Arrange
remaining slices of bread in overlapping
pattern over top.

Beat eggs in medium bowl. Stir in
milk, remaining 3/4 teaspoon salt and
hot pepper sauce. Pour gently over
bread. Sprinkle with remaining cheese.
Cover and chill at least 1 hour,
preferably overnight.

Bake uncovered at 375 degrees for
approximately 40 minutes.

Serves 6

Mexican Chili Cheese Puff

12 ounces Monterey Jack cheese, sliced
12 ounces sharp yellow Cheddar
    cheese, sliced
3 4-ounce cans whole green chilies,
    drained
1 12-ounce can evaporated milk
2 tablespoons flour
2 eggs, lightly beaten
1 cup sour cream (optional)

Preheat oven to 350 degrees.

Cut cheese slices into triangles. Slice
and seed the chilies. Starting with the
cheese, layer a 2-quart oval baking dish
with the cheese and chilies. Mix 1/4 cup
milk and flour to make a paste. Add
remaining milk and the beaten eggs
and mix well. Pour mixture over the
cheese and chilies. Bake for 45 minutes,
or until firm. Serve sour cream on the
side, if desired.

Serves 6-8

*A rich blend of eggs and cheese that will
become a favorite. Baked in a soufflé
dish, it is lovely enough to come right to
the table.*

Sausage and Cheese Strata
with Basil

1 pound bulk sausage
12 eggs, beaten
4 cups milk
1 teaspoon dry mustard
1 tablespoon fresh basil or 1 teaspoon
    dried
1/4 teaspoon pepper
10 slices white bread, crusts removed
    and cubed
2 cups shredded Cheddar cheese

Preheat oven to 350 degrees.

Brown sausage in medium skillet and
drain. Set aside. Mix eggs and milk.
Add dry mustard, basil and pepper.

Grease a 10 x 14-inch baking dish and
spread bread cubes over bottom. Cover
with sausage. Sprinkle 1½ cups
Cheddar cheese over sausage. Pour egg
mixture over cheese. Top with
remaining 1/2 cup cheese. Cover and
refrigerate overnight.

Bake strata for 50 minutes, or until
eggs are set and top is browned.

Serves 6-8

Souffléed Quiche

2 tablespoons butter
2 tablespoons minced shallots
1 clove garlic, minced
3/4 pound ham, minced
1/4 cup Madeira
3 eggs, separated
1 cup sour cream
1/4 cup fresh bread crumbs
1/4 cup grated Swiss cheese
1/2 teaspoon dried basil
1/8 teaspoon white pepper
1/8 teaspoon cream of tartar

Preheat oven to 400 degrees.

Melt butter in skillet. Add shallots, garlic and ham. Sauté, stirring frequently, until shallots are softened, about 3 minutes. Add Madeira. Cook, stirring until liquid evaporates, about 5 minutes. Cool.

Beat egg yolks in bowl until thickened. Stir in sour cream, bread crumbs, cheese, basil and pepper. Add cooled ham mixture.

Beat egg whites with cream of tartar until stiff. Fold into ham mixture. Pour into buttered quiche pan. Bake for 30 minutes or until puffed and lightly browned.

Serves 8

Quiche Wiki Wiki

1 9-inch baked pie shell
1/4 cup butter
1/4 cup chopped onion
1/4 cup chopped green pepper
1 beef bouillon cube
1 8-ounce can crushed pineapple, drain and reserve 1/2 cup juice
4 ounces shredded boiled ham
4 ounces grated Cheddar cheese
4 ounces grated Swiss cheese
4 eggs
1/2 cup evaporated milk
4 teaspoons brown mustard
1/4 teaspoon horseradish
1/4 teaspoon white pepper
Nutmeg

Preheat oven to 350 degrees.

In medium skillet, sauté onion and pepper in butter. Add bouillon cube and 1/2 cup pineapple juice. Simmer until liquid is absorbed. Add pineapple and ham. Blend. Spread in pie shell and top with cheeses. Blend eggs, milk, mustard, horseradish and white pepper and pour into pie shell. Sprinkle with nutmeg and bake for 35-40 minutes. Let stand for 10 minutes before cutting.

Serves 8

Spinach Phyllo Pie

2 10-ounce bags fresh spinach, washed, stems removed and dried or 3 10-ounce packages frozen chopped spinach, thawed and squeezed dry
2 tablespoons olive oil
2 bunches scallions, minced
5 eggs, beaten
1 pound feta cheese, crumbled
1 cup butter
1 1-pound package phyllo dough

Wash and dry the spinach the day before.

Preheat oven to 350 degrees.

Sauté the scallions in olive oil. Tear spinach into small pieces and place in mixing bowl. Add eggs, cheese and sautéed scallions.

Melt the butter. Coat a 9 x 13-inch pan with butter. Layer 5-10 sheets of phyllo, brushing butter between the sheets. Place spinach mixture on top. Again layer 5-10 sheets of phyllo, brushing butter between sheets. Heavily coat edges and top with butter. Score top layers of phyllo into large diagonal shapes. Bake for 1 hour or until golden brown.

Yields 30-40 bite-size pieces

Festive French Toast

3/4 cup butter, softened
1/3 cup sugar
2 teaspoons cinnamon
1/3 cup Southern Comfort

1 large loaf French bread
7 eggs
2 cups half and half

2 tablespoons butter
2 tablespoons oil
Hot maple syrup

Cream butter, sugar and cinnamon.
Beat in Southern Comfort. Slice bread
lengthwise and spread each half with
butter mixture. Replace to form loaf.
Cut into 1-inch slices and place on
high-sided cookie sheet.

Whisk eggs and half and half until
frothy and pour over bread slices. Chill
overnight, turning once.

Preheat a large skillet to a medium high
heat. Sauté bread slices in oil and
butter until golden. Serve with hot
maple syrup.

Serves 4-6

Orange Stuffed French Toast

16 ounces cream cheese, softened
2 teaspoons orange juice
1 teaspoon grated orange peel
1 cup chopped pecans

3 cups flour
4 teaspoons sugar
4 teaspoons baking powder
2 teaspoons salt
2 cups half and half
4 eggs, beaten

2 cups orange juice
1½ cups sugar
2 teaspoons grated orange peel
1 teaspoon cinnamon

1 loaf cinnamon raisin bread, sliced
    into 1-inch slices
1/2 cup vegetable oil

Filling: Mix together the cream cheese,
orange juice, orange peel and pecans;
set aside.

Batter: Sift together dry ingredients.
Add half and half and eggs and stir just
until blended.

Syrup: Boil orange juice and sugar until
syrupy. Add orange peel and cinnamon.

Make a pocket in each slice of bread
and divide the filling evenly among the
slices. Heat oil in a large skillet over
medium heat. Dip both sides of stuffed
bread slices in batter mixture and cook
in hot oil until browned. Serve with
orange syrup.

Serves 8

Pumpkin Waffles

2 cups flour
4 teaspoons baking powder
1/2 teaspoon coriander
1 tablespoon cinnamon
2 tablespoons sugar
1/2 teaspoon salt
1/2 teaspoon nutmeg
1 cup pumpkin purée
1½ cups milk
3/4 cup butter, melted
4 eggs, separated
1 tablespoon vanilla

Cider Syrup
1½ cups clear apple cider
1 cup brown sugar
1 cup light corn syrup
1 teaspoon grated lemon rind
1/8 teaspoon cinnamon
1/8 teaspoon nutmeg
Pinch ground cloves

Preheat waffle iron on high setting.
Mix flour, baking powder, coriander,
cinnamon, sugar, salt and nutmeg in a
large bowl. In a smaller bowl, combine
pumpkin, milk, melted butter, egg
yolks and vanilla. Pour over dry ingredients and mix just to blend. Beat egg
whites until stiff and fold into mixture.

Cider Syrup: Combine all ingredients
in a saucepan. Bring to a boil, then
reduce heat and simmer for 15 minutes. Keep warm.

Cook waffles on preheated waffle iron
and serve with butter and Cider Syrup.

Yields 6-8 waffles

Apple Popover Pancake

2 large apples, pared
2 tablespoons butter
2 tablespoons cinnamon sugar
3 eggs
3/4 cup milk
3/4 cup flour
1/2 teaspoon salt
Whipped cream (optional)

Preheat oven to 400 degrees.

Slice apples into sixteenths. Heat butter in an ovenproof round skillet. Add apple slices and sauté until softened. Sprinkle with 1 tablespoon cinnamon sugar mixture. Sauté over medium heat for 5 minutes.

Beat together eggs, milk, flour and salt. Pour mixture over apples in skillet. Place skillet in oven and bake for 20 minutes. Remove from oven, sprinkle with remaining cinnamon sugar and slice into 8 wedges. Serve immediately with a dollop of whipped cream.

Serves 8

Apples and pancakes come together in a unique way that will delight your family and friends. Have the breakfast plates warm and bring the popover to the table and slice into wedges.

Brie Soufflé

1/2 cup unsalted butter, softened
8 slices white bread, crusts removed
1 pound underripe brie, rind removed, cut into cubes
2 cups half and half
1 tablespoon chopped fresh dill
1 teaspoon salt
Dash hot pepper sauce
4 eggs

Butter one side of each slice of bread, then cut each slice into quarters. Arrange, buttered side up, on bottom of a buttered 1½-quart soufflé dish. Sprinkle evenly with half of the brie. Repeat, using remaining bread and brie. The soufflé may be covered and refrigerated for up to 24 hours at this point.

One hour before serving, whisk together half and half, dill, salt, hot pepper sauce and eggs. Preheat oven to 350 degrees. Pour egg mixture over bread and brie and let stand at room temperature for 30 minutes.

Bake for 30 minutes or until bubbling and golden brown.

Serves 8-10

Sweet and Cheesy Noodle Ring

12 ounces broad egg noodles
3 eggs, slightly beaten
8 whole pecans

3/4 cup brown sugar
1 teaspoon water
2 tablespoons butter

2 tablespoons butter, melted
1/2 cup sugar
1/2 teaspoon salt
1 tart apple, pared and chopped
1½ teaspoons cinnamon
1 cup chopped pecans
Juice of 1 lemon

Preheat oven to 350 degrees.

Cook noodles. Rinse well, drain and mix with eggs in a large bowl.

Generously grease a 9½-inch tube pan. Place whole pecans around bottom. Combine brown sugar, water and 2 tablespoons butter in saucepan. Bring to a boil and cook for 30 seconds. Pour into prepared pan.

In a smaller bowl, mix melted butter, sugar, salt, apple, cinnamon, pecans and lemon juice. Mix with noodle mixture and place into mold. (Recipe may be refrigerated at this point. Bring to room temperature before baking.) Bake for 45 minutes. Remove from oven and invert onto serving platter.

Serves 8

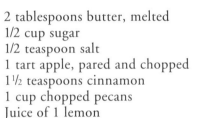

Super Bowl Boule

1 cup sour cream
1/2 envelope dry onion soup mix
2 tablespoons chopped, pitted black
    olives
2 tablespoons chopped sweet pickles or
    sweet pickle relish
1 9-inch round French bread loaf
Lettuce
12 ounces cooked roast beef, thinly
    sliced
4 ounces sliced Swiss cheese
1 tomato, sliced
1 green pepper, cut into rings

In a small bowl, combine sour cream,
onion soup mix, olives and pickles.
Chill 2 hours.

Cut a thin lengthwise slice off the top
of the bread loaf, reserving the top.
Hollow out the center of the loaf, leaving at least a 1/4-inch shell.

Spread 3/4 cup sour cream inside bread
shell. Line shell with lettuce and layer
with the roast beef, Swiss cheese, tomato slices, and pepper rings, spreading
remaining sour cream mixture between
each layer, except the top. Replace the
reserved top of loaf.

To serve, cut loaf in half, and again
into quarters.

Serves 4

Curried Sandwiches

2 3-ounce packages cream cheese with
    chives
1 tablespoon lemon juice
1 1/2 teaspoons curry powder
8 medium hearth rolls, split
1 pound ham or turkey, thinly sliced
6 ounces Swiss cheese, sliced
Pimento stuffed olives, halved

Preheat oven to 350 degrees.

In a small bowl, mix together cream
cheese, lemon juice, and curry powder.
Spread mixture on one side of each roll.

Divide the ham or turkey among the
rolls and top with the Swiss cheese.
Place top of the roll on each sandwich
and skewer with toothpicks garnished
with the olive halves. Wrap each
sandwich in foil and bake at 350
degrees for 10 minutes.

Serves 8

Shaved Ham Oven Sandwiches

1/2 cup butter, room temperature
2 tablespoons Dijon mustard
1 1/2 tablespoons poppy seeds
1 1/4 teaspoons Worcestershire sauce
1/2 medium onion, finely grated
8 Cracked Pepper Sandwich Rolls, split
1 pound shaved boiled ham
8 slices Swiss cheese

Preheat oven to 400 degrees.

Mix together butter, mustard, poppy
seeds, Worcestershire sauce, and onion.
Spread mixture thinly on both sides of
the 8 rolls. Divide the ham between the
rolls and top each with 1 slice of Swiss
cheese.

Wrap sandwiches in aluminum foil and
warm at 400 degrees for 10 minutes, or
until cheese melts.

Serves 8

Eggplant Roll-Ups

1 medium eggplant
1 egg, beaten
2 cups bread crumbs
2 tablespoons olive oil

2 cups ricotta cheese
1½ cups grated mozzarella cheese
Salt and pepper to taste
1 tablespoon parsley
3½ cups tomato sauce, preferably
    homemade

Preheat oven to 350 degrees.

Peel and slice eggplant lengthwise into
1/4-inch slices. Dip each in beaten egg
and then in bread crumbs. Sauté in
olive oil over medium heat until lightly
browned.

In a medium bowl, combine ricotta,
3/4 cup mozzarella, salt, pepper and
parsley. Place a spoonful of the cheese
mixture at the narrow end of the
eggplant slice and roll up.

Spread 1½ cups of tomato sauce evenly in the bottom of a lightly buttered
9 x 13-inch pan. Top with eggplant
roll-ups. Cover with remaining tomato
sauce and sprinkle with remaining mozzarella. Bake for 20 minutes.

Serves 4-6

Sunrise Salad

1 head romaine lettuce
3 ripe avocados
3 medium oranges
1 fresh pineapple
2 pints fresh strawberries
1/4 cup sliced almonds, toasted

Dressing
1/2 cup mayonnaise
1/4 cup sour cream
1/4 cup chopped parsley
3 scallions, thinly sliced
1 tablespoon tarragon vinegar
1 teaspoon sugar
1/4 teaspoon dry mustard
1/8 teaspoon garlic powder
1/8 teaspoon salt
Freshly ground pepper
1 3-ounce package cream cheese
Grated rind of 1 orange
2 teaspoons fresh lemon juice

Mix together mayonnaise, sour cream,
parsley, scallions, vinegar, sugar and
spices. Separately, cream together
cream cheese, orange rind and lemon
juice. Beat in mayonnaise mixture.

To serve, line a shallow bowl or platter
with torn romaine lettuce leaves. On
top, arrange sliced avocados, peeled
orange slices, fresh pineapple slices and
sliced strawberries. Bring dressing to
room temperature and pour over salad.
Top with toasted almonds.

Serves 8-10

Poppy Seed Tea Loaf

1 12-ounce can evaporated milk
1½ cups salad oil
4 eggs
1 teaspoon vanilla
3 cups flour
2 cups sugar
1/2 teaspoon baking soda
1/2 teaspoon salt
1/2 cup poppy seeds

Preheat oven to 350 degrees.

Combine milk, oil, eggs and vanilla in
a large bowl. Beat well with electric
mixer. Add remaining dry ingredients.
Beat at medium speed for about 3 minutes. Pour batter into three ungreased
8½ x 4½-inch loaf pans, filling about
1/2 to 2/3 full. Bake until tops are golden
and cracked and tester comes out clean,
40-45 minutes. Test with toothpick for
doneness. Cool on rack. Serve warm,
cold or toasted with butter.

Yields 3 loaves

*The first loaf will be eaten warm from
the oven. Wrap the others with ribbons
and deliver them to friends.*

Rum Raisin Sticky Buns

1/4 cup warm water
1 package dry yeast
1 teaspoon sugar
1 cup milk, scalded and cooled to
  lukewarm
2 tablespoons sugar
1 teaspoon salt
4 tablespoons butter
4½ cups flour
2 eggs, beaten

Filling
3 tablespoons butter
2 tablespoons sugar
1/2 teaspoon cinnamon

Topping
1 cup golden raisins
1/3 cup dark rum
8 tablespoons butter
1/2 cup dark corn syrup
1 cup dark brown sugar
1/2 teaspoon cinnamon
1/4 teaspoon nutmeg
1/4 teaspoon allspice
1 cup chopped pecans

Stir the yeast and sugar into the warm water; allow to become bubbly. Combine the milk, sugar, salt and butter; stir until butter is melted. Mix 2 cups of the flour with the yeast mixture. Stir in eggs. Add milk mixture and 2 more cups of flour. Stir well. Turn out onto floured surface and knead remaining 1/2 cup of flour into dough. Knead until smooth and no longer sticky. Place dough in a clean bowl, cover and allow to rise until doubled.

While dough is rising, soak raisins in rum. In a saucepan, combine the butter, syrup, sugar and spices for the topping. Heat until butter has melted, then stir. In a well buttered 9 x 13-inch pan, spoon in topping, nuts and soaked raisins.

After dough has risen, punch down. On a well-floured surface, roll into a rectangle, about 12 x 20 inches. Spread with filling. Roll in jelly roll fashion, 20 inches in length. Cut into 1-inch slices. Place in prepared pan, cut side up. Cover with plastic wrap that has been dusted with flour. Allow buns to rise and double in size and fill the pan.

Preheat oven to 375 degrees. Bake until light brown, approximately 20-25 minutes. Remove from oven and invert immediately onto serving dish.

Yields 20 buns

Filled with rum-soaked golden raisins, these breakfast buns are simply delectable. Serve warm from the oven.

Raspberry Crisp

3 medium apples, pared and sliced
2 cups raspberries
3/4 cup sugar
1/2 cup chopped walnuts

1 cup oatmeal
1/2 cup butter
1/3 cup flour
1 cup brown sugar

Preheat oven to 350 degrees.

Place apples in deep, greased 2-quart casserole. Mix raspberries, sugar and walnuts and add to casserole.

Blend oatmeal, butter, flour and sugar until crumbly. Top crisp with crumb mixture. Bake for 30 minutes.

Hint: Cranberries may be substituted when raspberries are not in season.

Serves 8

Pecan Topped Coffee Cake

2/3 cup butter
1 cup sugar
1/2 cup light brown sugar
2 eggs
1 teaspoon vanilla
2 cups flour
1 teaspoon baking powder
1 teaspoon baking soda
1/2 teaspoon salt
3/4 teaspoon cinnamon
1 cup buttermilk

Topping
1 cup chopped pecans
1/2 cup dark brown sugar
1/2 teaspoon cinnamon

Cream the butter and sugars, beating well. Add the eggs, beating well after each addition. Stir in vanilla. Combine the dry ingredients. Add to the creamed mixture alternately with the buttermilk, beginning and ending with the flour mixture. Mix well. Pour batter into greased and floured 9 x 13-inch pan. Combine topping ingredients and sprinkle over batter. Cover and chill 8-10 hours or overnight. Uncover batter and allow to come to room temperature. Preheat oven to 350 degrees. Bake cake until golden and tester inserted in center comes out clean, about 35 minutes.

Serves 10-12

Golden Sugar Puffs

2 cups flour
1/4 cup sugar
3 teaspoons baking powder
1 teaspoon salt
1 teaspoon nutmeg
1/4 cup salad oil
3/4 cup milk
1 egg
Oil
Cinnamon and sugar

Mix together flour, sugar, baking powder, salt and nutmeg. Combine the oil, milk and egg and add to the flour mixture. With a fork, stir until well mixed.

In a skillet, heat 2 inches of oil to 375 degrees. Drop teaspoons of dough into the oil and cook until golden brown, about 3 minutes, turning once. Drain well on paper towels. Roll in a cinnamon sugar mixture.

Yields 24 puffs

These Golden Sugar Puffs are so easy to prepare and so delicious! Stir together the batter in minutes, cook them until they are golden and serve them just as they come out of the cinnamon sugar.

Cranberry Coffee Cake

8 tablespoons butter, softened
1 cup sugar
2 eggs, unbeaten
1 teaspoon baking powder
1 teaspoon baking soda
1/2 teaspoon salt
2 cups flour
1 cup sour cream
1/2 teaspoon almond extract
1 cup whole cranberry sauce, fresh or canned
1/2 cup chopped walnuts

Glaze
3/4 cup confectioners sugar
2 tablespoons warm water
1/2 teaspoon vanilla

Preheat oven to 350 degrees.

Cream butter and sugar. Gradually add the eggs. Mix well. Combine the dry ingredients and add alternately with the sour cream and almond extract. Grease and flour a tube pan. Spread 1/2 of the batter in pan. Then add 1/2 the cranberry sauce on top of batter. Repeat with remaining batter and sauce, ending with the sauce on the top. Bake for 55 minutes.

Glaze: Combine sugar, water and vanilla and mix well.

Remove coffee cake from pan and cool 5 minutes. Spoon glaze over the cake. The secret of this coffee cake is not to let it dry out by overbaking.

Yields 10-12 slices

Pumpkin Pecan Bake

29 ounces pumpkin purée, fresh or
    canned
1/3 cup brown sugar
5 tablespoons butter, melted
1/2 teaspoon salt
1/2 teaspoon nutmeg
1/2 teaspoon cinnamon
1/2 teaspoon ginger
3 eggs, well beaten
2 tablespoons honey
1/2 cup light cream or evaporated milk
1/2 cup chopped pecans

Preheat oven to 375 degrees.

Mix together pumpkin purée, brown
sugar, butter, salt and spices. Stir in
eggs, honey and cream. Spoon into
greased 2-quart soufflé dish. Sprinkle
with pecans. Bake 50 minutes until
cooked through and slightly puffed.

Serves 4-6

*A creamy pumpkin purée sweetened with
honey and topped with toasted pecans
that is a beautiful addition to a Sunday
morning brunch or a holiday buffet.*

Baked Cream Spinach
in Tomatoes

5 10-ounce packages frozen chopped
    spinach
3 cups sliced mushrooms
3 tablespoons butter
3/4 cup sour cream
3/4 cup heavy cream
2 tablespoons dried minced onion
1 cup freshly grated Parmesan cheese
1 tablespoon horseradish
1 teaspoon nutmeg
1 teaspoon crushed red pepper flakes
    (optional)
1/2 teaspoon salt
1/2 teaspoon pepper
12 whole tomatoes
1/3 cup Parmesan cheese

Preheat oven to 350 degrees.

Cook spinach, drain and squeeze dry.
Sauté mushrooms in butter until soft,
5-7 minutes. Drain off excess liquid. In
a large bowl, combine spinach, mushrooms, sour cream, cream, minced onion, 1 cup Parmesan cheese, horseradish, nutmeg, red pepper flakes, salt and
pepper.

Cut top 1/4 to 1/3 off tomatoes. Core
out the seeds and juice, leaving the
pulp and exterior skin. Fill a 9 x 13-
inch baking pan with 1/2 inch of water.
Stuff tomatoes with spinach mixture
and place in baking pan. Bake for 25
minutes. Sprinkle with 1/3 cup of Parmesan cheese and bake for an additional 10-15 minutes.

Serves 12

Cranberry Filled Acorn Squash

1 large acorn squash
1 teaspoon cornstarch
1/4 cup apple cider
1 ½ cups cranberries
1/4 cup sugar
1/8 teaspoon ground cloves
1/4 teaspoon ground nutmeg
1 tablespoon chopped pecans or
    walnuts

Cut squash in half lengthwise. Remove
seeds and fibers. In a covered saucepan,
steam squash in 1 inch of water until
soft, 10-15 minutes. Remove from water and set aside.

Preheat oven to 375 degrees.

Mix cornstarch with 2 tablespoons of
cider; set aside. Combine remaining
cider, cranberries and spices in a
1-quart saucepan. Cook over medium
high heat until cranberry skin pops.
Stir in cornstarch mixture. Cook until
thickened. Spoon cranberry mixture
into squash and sprinkle nuts on top.
Cover with foil and heat squash in oven
until thoroughly heated, about 15
minutes.

Serves 6

Pasta

Linguini with Scallops and Snow Peas

3/4 pound fresh linguini
1/4 cup butter, melted
5 tablespoons butter
2 cloves garlic, minced
1/2 pound bay scallops
1/2 pound medium shrimp, peeled and deveined
1 teaspoon salt
1 teaspoon pepper
2 cups snow peas, blanched
3/4 cup grated Parmesan cheese

Cook linguini. Drain and toss with 1/4 cup butter.

Heat remaining 5 tablespoons of butter in a large skillet. Add garlic and sauté until softened. Add scallops, shrimp, salt and pepper. Sauté 3-4 minutes, or until shrimp and scallops are opaque. Add snow peas and heat through. Toss mixture with linguini, add cheese and serve at once.

Serves 4-6

Linguini with Brie

2/3 cup light olive oil
1 cup packed chopped fresh basil
3 cloves garlic, minced
1 teaspoon salt
1/2 teaspoon pepper
4 large ripe tomatoes, peeled and chopped
1 pound brie
1¼ pounds fresh linguini
Parmesan cheese

Add olive oil, basil, garlic, salt and pepper to chopped tomatoes. Mix and let stand, covered, at room temperature for 1 hour (or refrigerate overnight and bring to room temperature before using).

Remove rind from brie and cut cheese into small pieces.

Cook linguini. Drain but do not rinse. Toss immediately with brie until cheese has melted. Add tomato mixture and toss. Sprinkle with Parmesan cheese to taste.

Serves 8

Ripe tomatoes are what give this dish its colorful appeal. Accompany with loaves of hot French Bread and finish with Coffee Tortoni with Chocolate Sauce.

Zesty Linguini with Vodka and Rosy Tomato Sauce

2 tablespoons olive oil
3 tablespoons butter
1 small onion, chopped
1 clove garlic, minced
1 28-ounce can plum tomatoes
1 tablespoon chopped fresh basil
1/8 teaspoon dried red pepper or
   1/8 teaspoon cayenne, to taste
1/2 cup vodka
1/2 cup heavy cream
3 tablespoons Parmesan cheese
12 ounces fresh linguini
Freshly ground pepper
Parsley

Sauté onion in butter and oil in medium skillet for about 5 minutes. Add garlic and sauté another minute. Add tomatoes, basil, red pepper and vodka. Simmer about 15 minutes until sauce is reduced. Add cream and simmer until thickened, about 5 minutes more. Add Parmesan cheese and blend well.

Cook pasta, then drain. Layer sauce on plate, then add pasta, then add more sauce. Garnish with pepper and parsley.

Serves 4

White Lasagna with Shrimp and Broccoli

Sauce
1/2 cup butter
2 cloves garlic, minced
1/2 cup flour
1/4 teaspoon salt
1/4 teaspoon Italian seasoning
2 cups milk
2 cups chicken broth

8 ounces lasagna noodles, cooked and drained
2 cups part skim ricotta cheese
1½ pounds shrimp, peeled and deveined
2 cups broccoli florets, steamed
8 ounces mozzarella cheese, sliced
1 cup grated Parmesan cheese

Sauce: Heat butter in 3-quart saucepan over low heat until melted. Add garlic. Stir in flour, salt and Italian seasoning. Cook briefly, stirring constantly. Stir in milk and broth. Heat to boiling, stirring constantly. Cook 1 minute more. Turn heat to low.

Preheat oven to 350 degrees.

Spread 1/4 of the sauce in an ungreased 9 x 13-inch baking dish. Top with 3 or 4 lasagna noodles. Spread 1/3 of the ricotta cheese, shrimp and broccoli over noodles. Top with 1/3 of the mozzarella cheese and more sauce. Sprinkle with 1/3 of the Parmesan cheese. Repeat layers 2 times, ending with sauce. Cover with foil and bake for 35 minutes.

Serves 8-10

Light Style Stuffed Shells

Sauce
3 tablespoons olive oil
3/4 cup chopped onion
2 cloves garlic, minced
2 tablespoons chopped fresh basil
3 28-ounce cans peeled tomatoes, crushed
Salt and pepper to taste

1 12-ounce package jumbo pasta shells

Filling
1 10-ounce package frozen chopped spinach, thawed and squeezed dry
2 pounds part-skim ricotta cheese
1 cup shredded part-skim mozzarella cheese
Pepper to taste

Sauce: In large pan, sauté onion and garlic in oil. Add basil, tomatoes, salt and pepper. Simmer 15 minutes.

Cook pasta shells according to package directions.

Filling: In a large bowl, combine spinach, ricotta, 3/4 cup of the mozzarella cheese and pepper. Blend well.

Preheat oven to 350 degrees. Stuff each shell with ample cheese mixture. Spread half of the sauce in a baking dish. Put shells on top and spoon more sauce on top. Sprinkle with remaining mozzarella. Bake shells for 30 minutes or until heated through.

Serves 8-10

Tortellini Alfredo

1 pound fresh tortellini, meat or cheese
1/4 cup unsalted butter
2 cloves garlic, finely minced
2 tablespoons chopped fresh parsley
1/2 cup half and half
Dash salt and pepper
1/3 cup finely grated Parmesan cheese

Cook tortellini and drain.

In a medium skillet, sauté garlic in butter until golden, being careful not to brown. Add parsley, half and half, salt and pepper and continue cooking over medium heat until very hot, but not boiling. Add cheese and stir over heat for about 3 minutes, being careful not to let it boil. Season to taste with salt and pepper.

Toss tortellini with sauce and garnish with Parmesan cheese.

Serves 4

Fresh tortellini is the secret to this delectable pasta dish. Bathed in a warm cream sauce and topped with lots of freshly grated Parmesan cheese, this dish is ambrosia.

Pasta Primavera

1 pound rotelli pasta
1/3 cup olive oil

1/2 cup chopped red onion
3/4 pound snow peas, blanched
1/3 pound zucchini, julienne and
    steamed
2 red peppers, julienne
1/2 cup chopped chives
Grated orange peel of 1 medium orange
1 cup pitted black olives
1/3 cup grated Parmesan cheese
4 tablespoons raspberry vinegar
Cherry tomatoes and scallions for
    garnish

Cook pasta; drain.

Toss cooked pasta, while still warm,
with the olive oil. Set aside.

Mix together the onion, snow peas,
zucchini, red peppers, chives, orange
peel, olives, Parmesan cheese and
vinegar and toss with pasta. May be
served warm or cold. Garnish with
cherry tomatoes and scallions prior to
serving.

Hint: The longer this dish sits, the
better it tastes.

Serves 8

Fettucine Carbonara

1 pound fresh spinach fettucine
1 pound bacon
1 cup butter, softened
1 cup grated Parmesan cheese
6 eggs, lightly beaten
2 cups half and half
Salt and pepper

Cook fettucine; drain.

Cook bacon until crisp. Drain and
crumble. Beat butter and cheese until
combined. Gradually beat eggs into
butter and cheese mixture. Stir in half
and half. Place mixture in a large
saucepan and heat but do not boil.

Add fettucine and toss. Sprinkle bacon
on top and salt and pepper to taste.
Serve immediately.

Serves 6-8

Fettucine and Plum Tomatoes

1 pound fresh fettucine
12 plum tomatoes, peeled, chopped
2 tablespoons packed, chopped fresh
    basil
1/4 cup olive oil
2-3 cloves garlic, minced
1/2 cup grated Parmesan cheese

Cook fettucine; drain.

Combine tomatoes, basil, olive oil and
garlic and toss with pasta.

Serve warm or at room temperature,
dusted with Parmesan cheese.

Serves 6

*Perfect for a picnic or an outdoor
brunch. Arrange on a large colorful
platter and surround with fresh basil
leaves.*

Spinach Pasta with Shrimp

1 pound spinach fettucine
1 pound medium shrimp
1/4 pound bacon
1½ cups heavy cream
1/4 pound Gorgonzola cheese
1/2 teaspoon nutmeg
Freshly ground pepper to taste

Cook fettucini; drain.

Cook shrimp in boiling water for about 5 minutes until pink in color. Cool in pan of cold water. Peel and devein.

Cook bacon in frying pan, crumble and set aside.

In a large saucepan, stir cream over low heat until slightly thickened. Cut cheese into small pieces and add to cream. Add nutmeg and pepper and stir until cheese melts. Add shrimp and bacon, then toss with fettucine. Garnish with additional nutmeg.

Serves 6-8

Vermicelli with Vegetables

2/3 cup chicken broth
2½ tablespoons cornstarch
3 tablespoons dry sherry
1/2 teaspoon salt
1/4 cup plus 2 tablespoons soy sauce
1/4 teaspoon hot pepper sauce
1/4 teaspoon dried ginger
1 teaspoon sugar
4 tablespoons salad oil
8 ounces vermicelli, cooked al dente, drained
4 scallions, cut into 1/2-inch slices
2 garlic cloves, minced
1 cup asparagus, cut into 1-inch pieces, blanched
1/2 cup julienne red pepper
3/4 cup broccoli florets, blanched

In medium bowl, combine chicken broth, cornstarch, sherry, salt, soy sauce, hot pepper sauce, ginger and sugar; set aside.

In heavy skillet or wok, heat 2 tablespoons oil until very hot, but not smoking. Add vermicelli and cook, stirring frequently and quickly over high heat for 3 minutes. Remove from pan. Add 1 tablespoon oil and heat. Add scallions and garlic and stir fry 30 seconds. Add remaining tablespoon oil and heat. Add asparagus, red pepper and broccoli. Stir fry 3 minutes. Add soy sauce mixture and stir until sauce thickens. Pour over hot vermicelli and toss.

Serves 4

Red Pepper Cappellini

2 tablespoons oil
1/2 cup finely diced lean salt pork, thick rind removed
3 cloves garlic, minced
1/2 teaspoon red pepper flakes
3 tablespoons butter
1 tablespoon fresh chopped parsley
Freshly ground pepper
8 ounces cappellini

In a medium skillet, heat oil. Add salt pork and sauté until browned and crisped. Remove with slotted spoon and set aside. In the same skillet, sauté the garlic over low heat until limp. Increase heat to medium and add the red pepper flakes, butter, parsley and pepper. Stir until the butter is melted.

In a large pot, cook cappellini al dente. Drain and toss with the salt pork and the butter mixture. Serve immediately.

Serves 4

Strata Florentine with Shrimp

Red Sauce
3 tablespoons olive oil
2 onions, finely chopped
2 cloves garlic, minced
1 28-ounce can crushed tomatoes
1 6-ounce can tomato paste
1 tablespoon chopped fresh basil
1 tablespoon chopped fresh parsley
Salt and pepper to taste

Cream Sauce
5 tablespoons butter
3 medium shallots, minced
5 tablespoons flour
2½ cups milk
1/2 cup dry vermouth
Dash red pepper

Vegetable Layer
3 tablespoons olive oil
1 pound zucchini, diced
1 onion, chopped
2 cloves garlic, minced
2 green peppers, diced
3 tablespoons chopped fresh basil
Salt and pepper to taste

Cheese and Spinach Layer
2 10-ounce packages frozen chopped
    spinach
1½ pounds ricotta cheese
1 egg, beaten
3 tablespoons Pernod liqueur
1/2 teaspoon ground nutmeg

15 lasagna noodles, cooked and drained
1½ pounds medium shrimp, peeled and
    deveined
1/4 cup grated Parmesan cheese

Red Sauce: Sauté onions and garlic in olive oil. Add the tomatoes, tomato paste and herbs. Salt and pepper to taste. Simmer for 10-15 minutes.

Cream Sauce: Cook shallots in butter over low heat. Stir in flour. Keep stirring while pouring in the milk and vermouth. Mix until thickened. Season the sauce with red pepper and remove from heat.

Vegetable Layer: Sauté the zucchini, onion, garlic and pepper in olive oil until softened. Add the basil. Salt and pepper to taste.

Cheese and Spinach Layer: Cook the spinach according to package directions and drain. Mix spinach with cheese, egg, Pernod and nutmeg.

Assemble the strata in a 9 x 13-inch baking dish. Preheat oven to 350 degrees. Spread most of the red sauce on the bottom of the pan, then place 3 noodles on top of the sauce. Add the vegetable layer, then 3 more noodles. Spread cream sauce over noodles and place raw shrimp on top of sauce. Add 3 more noodles, then the spinach and cheese mixture. Add remaining noodles, then pour remaining sauce on top. Sprinkle with Parmesan cheese. Bake for 45 minutes.

Serves 10-12

Fettucine à l'Orange

8 ounces fresh egg fettucine
2 teaspoons cornstarch
1 cup orange juice
4 teaspoons butter
3 small carrots, cut into 2-inch
    matchsticks
16 medium shrimp, peeled, deveined
    and sliced lengthwise
1 cup snow peas
1 teaspoon salt
1/2 cup enoki mushrooms
Fresh chives
Freshly ground pepper

Cook fettucine al dente; drain.

Blend cornstarch and orange juice together in a small bowl; set aside.

In a heavy skillet, melt butter and sauté carrots 1 minute. Add shrimp and sauté until they curl and become opaque. Add snow peas, and sauté another minute. Stir in orange sauce. Boil until sauce thickens, about 1 minute. Stir in salt. Remove from heat and stir in mushrooms.

Toss pasta with sauce, and garnish with a handful of fresh chives and black pepper.

Serves 4

A light and festive entrée that is a feast for the eyes as well as the palate.

Oriental Beef and Linguini

1 pound flank steak
8 ounces linguini
2 tablespoons salad oil
1 bunch broccoli, approximately
    1½ pounds
1 pound fresh asparagus

Dressing
1/2 cup soy sauce
1/2 cup less 2 tablespoons safflower oil
3 tablespoons sesame oil
1½-inch piece fresh ginger, grated
2 cloves garlic, minced
1/4 teaspoon salt
1/2 teaspoon freshly ground pepper
1 teaspoon sugar
1-2 tablespoons minced scallions

Grill or broil flank steak to medium rare. Cool and thinly slice. Cook pasta until al dente, drain well and toss with 2 tablespoons of salad oil.

Remove stalks from broccoli. Break the florets into bite-size pieces. Blanch for 30 seconds; rinse under cold water. Break off end of asparagus and cut into bite-size pieces. Blanch for 30 seconds; rinse under cold water.

Dressing: Whisk together soy sauce, oils, ginger, garlic, salt, pepper, sugar and scallions.

Toss the beef with approximately 1/2 cup of the dressing and let it marinate briefly. Put the pasta, meat and vegetables into a large bowl. Toss with remaining dressing. Serve at room temperature or slightly chilled.

Serves 8

The taste of the Orient is in the dressing which is seasoned with soy, sesame oil and fresh ginger. It marinates the thin slices of grilled flank steak and lightly coats the tender fresh asparagus and broccoli as it is tossed into the perfect main dish pasta salad.

Festive Pasta with Garlic Mayonnaise

2 cups mayonnaise
2 cloves garlic, minced
2 6-ounce jars marinated artichoke
    hearts, drained and sliced (reserve
    oil)
1 pound spirelli or rotelli pasta
2 whole boneless chicken breasts
1 8-ounce can hearts of palm, drained
    and sliced
4 heads Belgian endive, leaves separated
Pink peppercorns as garnish

Combine mayonnaise with garlic and oil drained from artichoke hearts. Chill.

Cook pasta according to package directions and rinse in cold water. Place in large bowl and bring to room temperature. Stir to keep from sticking. Blend 1/3 garlic flavored mayonnaise with pasta. Chill overnight to allow flavors to blend. Remove from refrigerator 30 minutes before serving.

Poach chicken in water until opaque and cut into bite-size pieces. Combine artichoke hearts, hearts of palm, chicken and remaining mayonnaise. Chill overnight if desired.

To serve, line plates with endive leaves. Spoon pasta atop lower half of leaves and arrange artichoke mixture on pasta. Garnish with pink peppercorns.

Serves 6-8

Tortellini Salad

1 pound green tortellini
1 pound white tortellini
1 small head cauliflower, cut into
     florets
1 small bunch broccoli, cut into florets
2 green zucchini, sliced and cut into
     quarters
2 yellow summer squash, sliced and cut
     into quarters
1 yellow pepper, diced
1 red pepper, diced
1/2 can pitted black medium olives, cut
     in half
1 3-ounce package French goat cheese

Dressing
2 ounces anchovy fillets
1 teaspoon minced garlic
1 tablespoon Dijon mustard
1/4 cup red wine vinegar
1 egg yolk
1/2 cup light olive oil
1/2 cup soybean oil
Parmesan cheese
Salt and pepper to taste

Cook pasta and drain; toss lightly with
a small amount of dressing and let cool.

Blanch the vegetables and remove while
still crunchy; rinse with cold water and
drain.

Dressing: Mash anchovy fillets;
combine with garlic, mustard, vinegar
and egg yolk. Slowly add oil, whisking
constantly until thickened. Add
Parmesan cheese, salt and pepper to
taste.

To serve, toss vegetables with pasta in a
large bowl. Add olives and crumbled
goat cheese. Gently blend in salad
dressing to taste.

Serves 10-12

*A colorful array of garden vegetables
amid the green and white tortellini
provides a spectacular dish for a summer
party. Choose cheese tortellini for a
luncheon or meat tortellini for a casual
supper.*

Chicken and Broccoli Pasta

4 boneless skinless chicken breast
     halves
3 cups broccoli florets
8 ounces spiral pasta
1/2 cup chopped walnuts
1/2 cup grated fresh Parmesan cheese
1 tablespoon lemon juice
1 teaspoon dried basil
1/4 cup mayonnaise

Poach chicken in water until opaque,
about 25 minutes. Cool and shred into
bite-size pieces. Steam broccoli until
crisp; rinse with cold water; drain.
Cook pasta al dente; drain; rinse with
cold water and drain again.

Place chicken, broccoli and pasta in a
large bowl. Combine remaining
ingredients and stir into chicken
mixture. Chill 2 hours or overnight to
allow flavors to blend.

Serves 4-6

Shrimp and Linguini Salad

2 pounds unpeeled medium shrimp
1 pound linguini
9 ounces fresh snow peas
6 scallions, chopped
6 medium tomatoes, peeled, chopped
3/4 cup walnut or olive oil
1/2 cup finely chopped parsley
1/3 cup raspberry or wine vinegar
1 teaspoon dried oregano
1 1/2 teaspoons basil
3/4 teaspoon garlic salt
3/4 teaspoon coarsely ground black
    pepper

Bring a pot of water to boil; add
shrimp and cook 3 minutes. Drain,
chill, peel and devein. Set aside.

Cook linguini al dente. Drain; rinse
with cold water and drain again.

Combine linguini, shrimp, and all
other ingredients. Toss gently. Cover
and chill for at least 2 hours.

Serves 10-12

Pasta and Spinach Salad

with Aioli

1 pound Mostacciolor (shell pasta)
4 cups spinach, cut into 1 1/2-inch strips
1 cup julienne red pepper
1 cup frozen green peas or pea pods,
    thawed
1 13-ounce can artichoke hearts,
    drained
1/2 teaspoon salt
1/4 teaspoon pepper

Dressing
1 cup mayonnaise, preferably
    homemade
5 small cloves garlic, minced
2 tablespoons lemon juice
2 teaspoons Dijon mustard

Cook pasta al dente; drain; rinse with
cold water and drain again.

To prepare salad, mix pasta, spinach,
red pepper, peas, artichokes, salt and
pepper. In a separate bowl, stir together
the dressing ingredients. Fold dressing
into the salad and serve.

Serves 8-12

Pasta Caesar Salad

8 ounces spirelli or rotelli pasta, cooked
    and drained
1 medium zucchini, cubed
2 ounces sun-dried tomatoes, blanched
    or already softened
1/2 red pepper, diced
2/3 cup pitted black olives, quartered

Dressing
2 ounces anchovy fillets
1 teaspoon minced garlic
1 tablespoon Dijon mustard
1/4 cup red wine vinegar
1 egg yolk
1/2 cup extra light olive oil
1/2 cup soybean oil
Salt and pepper to taste

3/4 cup toasted pine nuts
1/4 cup freshly grated Parmesan cheese

Cook pasta al dente; drain; rinse with
cold water and drain again.

Mix pasta with zucchini, tomatoes, red
pepper and olives. Chill.

Dressing: Mash anchovy fillets.
Combine with garlic, mustard, vinegar,
egg yolk, salt and pepper. Add oil
slowly, whisking constantly until
dressing thickens.

Toss salad with enough dressing to coat
thoroughly. Top with pine nuts and
Parmesan cheese.

Serves 8-10

Philadelphia's vibrant spirit comes alive through its events. Every January 1, Philadelphia rings in the new year with spectacular splashes of color, music and dance in the unique, centuries-old Mummers Day Parade. Costumed in feathers and sequins, some 25,000 Mummers pluck their banjos and strut their stuff up Broad Street in a parade that has come to be known as Philadelphia's Mardi Gras.

As the winter months wane, the Book and the Cook Fair teams the city's best chefs with outstanding cookbook authors to create a sumptuous festival of food. As spring arrives, the Philadelphia Flower Show, the nation's largest indoor flower exhibition, reminds us that the glory of this area's rich and fertile soil is right around the corner.

On October's Super Sunday, Philadelphia celebrates the city with dishes from virtually all ethnic backgrounds at a blockbuster block party on the Benjamin Franklin Parkway, our arrow-straight Champs Élysées-like boulevard.

The Academy Ball, the Philadelphia Antiques Show, the Zoobilee, the Philadelphia Craft Show, and the Foundation for Architecture's Beaux Arts Ball benefit our cultural and public institutions. In doing so, they reconfirm Philadelphia's long-time commitment to public support of its institutions and general philanthropy.

We believe, however, that the best events in Philadelphia can be found in private homes, experimenting with new foods, trying different table presentations, and entertaining good friends. We invite you to share this tradition.

Bon appétit, From Our Past To Your Presentation.

*The Beaux Arts Ball,
sponsored by
the Foundation for
Architecture, is
held every October in a
Philadelphia building
undergoing renovation.*

*The Annenberg Center's
Philadelphia International
Theatre Festival for
Children brings professional
theatre to over 30,000
Delaware Valley children
each May.*

*The Book and the Cook,
sponsored by the city,
teams up the city's best
chefs with outstanding
cookbook authors.*

*One of the events
during the week-long Freedom
Festival in July is the
Hot Air Balloon Race on
the Parkway.*

*Known as Philadelphia's
Mardi Gras, the
Mummers Day Parade
ushers in the
New Year with flash
and color.*

*The CoreStates Bike Race
whizzes past the
international flags lining
the Benjamin
Franklin Parkway.*

*The finale of the
Freedom Festival is the
fourth of July
fireworks over the
Philadelphia Museum
of Art.*

*Penn Relays—a premier
national track and field
event—is held at the
University of Pennsylvania's
Franklin Field.*

*The Devon Horse Show
and Country Fair,
the ultimate equestrian
event, benefits the
Bryn Mawr Hospital.*

Breads

Sesame Salt and Pepper Crackers

1/2 cup flour
1/4 to 1/2 teaspoon pepper, to taste
1/4 to 1/2 teaspoon salt, to taste
2 tablespoons butter
1 tablespoon sour cream
2 teaspoons water
2 tablespoons butter, melted
2 tablespoons sesame seeds

Preheat oven to 350 degrees.

Mix the flour, pepper and salt. Blend in the butter with a pastry blender until it is the consistency of cornmeal. Add the sour cream and water and mix to form a soft dough. On a floured surface, roll the dough very thin, about 1/8-inch thick. Cut into rounds with a 2-inch cookie cutter. Place on a lightly greased baking sheet. Brush with melted butter and sprinkle with sesame seeds. Bake until golden brown, 8-10 minutes.

Yields 14 crackers

These thin and crunchy crackers are topped with buttery, toasted sesame seeds and are a perfect complement to a cup of Black Bean Soup or a crock of Mostly Mushrooms.

Tangy Rye Sticks

3/4 cup milk, scalded
1 tablespoon butter
1¼ teaspoons salt
1½ teaspoons sugar
1/4 to 1/2 teaspoon cayenne pepper
   (adjust according to taste)
1 package dry yeast
1/4 cup warm water
1/2 cup rye flour
2 to 2¼ cups flour
1 egg, lightly beaten with 1 tablespoon
   water
Coarse salt

Combine first 5 ingredients in a large bowl. Stir and allow to cool to luke-warm. Dissolve yeast in warm water until bubbly, then add to the milk mixture. Add the rye flour and stir. Add the white flour and mix well to make a workable dough. Knead on a floured surface until the dough is smooth. Place in a clean, dry bowl, cover and allow to rise and double in volume, about 1 hour.

Divide the dough in half and roll into two 12-inch circles. Cut into 1½ to 2-inch wedges. Roll each wedge into straight crescents. Place on greased baking pans. Brush with egg mixture. Cover with plastic wrap that has been dusted with flour. Allow to rise and double.

Preheat oven to 400 degrees. Brush dough again with egg mixture and sprinkle with coarse salt. Bake until lightly browned, 12-14 minutes.

Yields 3 dozen

Italian Flat Bread

1 package dry yeast
1/4 cup warm water
1/2 teaspoon sugar
1/4 cup flour
1 teaspoon salt
3/4 cup warm water
2¼ cups flour
1½ tablespoons olive oil
1 teaspoon parsley
1 teaspoon sage
1 teaspoon oregano
1 teaspoon coarse salt

In a large mixer bowl, combine the yeast with the 1/4 cup warm water, sugar, flour and salt. Stir and allow to become bubbly. Add remaining water and flour, stirring well to mix. Turn onto a floured surface, kneading until smooth and no longer sticky. Place in a clean bowl, cover and allow to rise until doubled, about 1 hour.

Preheat oven to 450 degrees. Punch down dough. On a floured surface, roll into an oval about 11 x 13-inches and about 1-inch thick. Place on a floured baking sheet. Brush dough with olive oil, then sprinkle with spices and salt. Bake until golden brown, about 15-20 minutes. Cut into wedges to serve, warm or cool.

Yields 12 slices

Herb Butter French Bread
Herb Butter Bread Sticks

8 tablespoons butter
1/2 teaspoon garlic powder
1 teaspoon Jane's Crazy Mixed-Up Salt
1 teaspoon parsley flakes
1/2 teaspoon onion powder
1/2 teaspoon paprika
1/2 teaspoon oregano
Bread (see recipes below)
American or Provolone cheese

Combine butter with herbs and spices. Can be used in either recipe.

French Bread: Preheat oven to 350 degrees. Cut a wide loaf of French bread (about 14 ounces) lengthwise. Spread the entire butter mixture on both halves of the bread. Place slices of American or Provolone cheese on the bottom half of the bread, cutting them to fit. Place top of loaf over cheese-covered bottom. Slice entire loaf into 1-inch sections. Keep in loaf shape, wrap in aluminum foil and bake until cheese has melted, approximately 25 minutes.

Bread Sticks: Preheat oven to 250 degrees. Spread butter mixture onto thick, toasting style bread (entire loaf, 12-14 slices). Cut off the crusts and cut the bread into fourths. Place on a baking sheet. Bake for about 35 minutes. Turn off heat and leave in the oven overnight or for 8 hours. Store in cookie tins.

Yields 15 slices of French bread or 4½ dozen bread sticks

Cheese and Chive Biscuits

2 cups flour
1 tablespoon baking powder
1/2 teaspoon salt
2 teaspoons sugar
3 tablespoons butter
3/4 cup grated white Cheddar cheese
2 tablespoons chopped fresh chives
3/4 cup plus 1 tablespoon milk

Preheat oven to 425 degrees.

Mix flour, baking powder, salt and sugar. Add butter and mix with a fork until crumbly. Stir in cheese and chives. Add milk and stir quickly until dough sticks together. On a floured surface, gently knead dough a few times. Pat or roll out to 3/4 to 1-inch thick. Do not overmix. Cut into rounds with a floured cutter. Place on a greased baking sheet. Bake 12-15 minutes, until golden.

Yields 1 dozen biscuits

These flaky biscuits take on a new look and taste with the introduction of cheese and chives. Cut into different shapes for a festive touch.

Jalapeño Corn Bread

1 cup yellow cornmeal
1 cup flour
2 tablespoons sugar
1 teaspoon baking soda
2 teaspoons cream of tartar
1/4 teaspoon salt
1 cup sour cream
1/4 cup milk
2 eggs, well beaten
3 tablespoons butter, melted
2 tablespoons chopped, seeded and drained pickled jalapeño peppers (adjust according to taste)
1 cup grated Monterey Jack cheese

Preheat oven to 425 degrees.

Combine cornmeal, flour, sugar, soda, cream of tartar and salt and mix well. Add sour cream, milk, eggs, butter, peppers and cheese. Stir briefly, only to mix. Spoon into buttered 9 x 9-inch pan. Bake for 18-20 minutes, or until cake tester comes out clean when inserted in center. Cool briefly and cut into squares. Serve warm.

Yields 9 3-inch squares

Cracked Pepper Sandwich Rolls

1 cup boiling water
3 tablespoons butter
1½ tablespoons sugar
1¼ teaspoons salt
1 package dry yeast
1¼ teaspoons sugar
1/2 cup warm water
1 egg
3 to 4 cups flour
1 egg beaten with 1 tablespoon water
Coarse salt
Freshly ground black pepper

Mix first 4 ingredients and cool to lukewarm. Dissolve yeast with sugar in warm water and allow to become bubbly. Combine egg and 3 cups flour and mix with above ingredients. Knead, adding flour as necessary, until smooth and no longer sticky. Allow to rise in a clean bowl, covered, until doubled, about 1 hour.

Punch down and divide dough into about 8 pieces. Shape into 3-inch round shapes, stretching outside edges to bottom side. Flatten slightly. Place on a baking sheet which has been sprinkled with flour or cornmeal, about 2 inches apart. Cover with plastic wrap that has been dusted with flour. Allow to rise and double, about 30 minutes.

Preheat oven to 375 degrees. Carefully brush rolls with egg glaze. Sprinkle lightly with salt and generously with pepper. Bake for 15-20 minutes, until rolls are light brown and sound hollow when tapped.

Yields 8 large deli style rolls

Soft Pretzels

1 package dry yeast
1 scant tablespoon sugar
3/4 cup warm water
1/2 teaspoon salt
2 cups flour
4 cups water
4 tablespoons baking soda
Coarse salt

Dissolve yeast with sugar in warm water until bubbly; mix with salt and flour. Knead until dough becomes smooth. In a 9 to 10-inch skillet, dissolve the baking soda in the 4 cups water. Heat slowly until the water is simmering.

Preheat oven to 425 degrees. Separate the dough into 6 sections. Roll each piece into a long rope about 1/2 to 1-inch thick. Twist into pretzel shape. Gently submerge pretzels in simmering water for about 30 seconds. Remove with slotted spoon. Place pretzels on a well greased baking sheet that has been sprinkled with coarse salt. Sprinkle tops of pretzels with salt. Bake for 15 minutes or until golden brown. Recipe may be doubled.

Yields 6 pretzels

French Bread

1 cup warm water
1 package dry yeast
1½ teaspoons sugar
1½ teaspoons salt
2¼ to 2½ cups flour
Sesame seeds or poppy seeds (optional)

Dissolve yeast and sugar in warm water. Allow to become bubbly. Add salt and flour and mix well. Knead on floured surface until smooth and no longer sticky. Place in clean bowl, covered, and allow to rise until doubled.

Punch down and roll into a 10 x 17-inch rectangle. Roll into a long loaf, jelly roll fashion. With seam side down, place on well floured (corn meal may be used) 12 x 18-inch baking sheet. Slash top of bread diagonally with a sharp knife at 3-inch intervals. Cover with plastic wrap that has been dusted with flour and allow to double.

Fill spray bottle with warm water and on fine mist, spray unbaked loaf. At this point, sesame or poppy seeds may be sprinkled on top. Gently, place in a cold oven. Turn heat to 375 degrees. Continue spraying loaf at 3 minute intervals for about 12 minutes. Bake until loaf is golden brown and sounds hollow when tapped, 40-45 minutes. Place on rack to cool. Allow to cool before slicing.

Yields 1 loaf

Southern Dinner Rolls

1 package dry yeast
1/2 cup warm water
1/2 teaspoon sugar
1/3 cup sugar
5 tablespoons butter
1/2 teaspoon salt
1/2 cup boiling water
3 to 3½ cups flour
1 egg, beaten

Dissolve the yeast with the sugar in warm water. Allow to become bubbly. Combine the sugar, butter, salt and boiling water. Allow to cool. In a large bowl, add the flour, yeast mixture and egg and stir well. Add the cooled water mixture. Stir well. Turn onto a well floured surface. Knead until smooth and no longer sticky. Place in a clean, dry bowl, cover and allow to rise until doubled. Punch down and allow to rise for another 30 minutes. Punch down again. The dough may be shaped into either of the following rolls:

Parkerhouse Rolls: Roll out dough on a floured surface to about 1/4-inch thickness. Cut into 3-inch circles. Brush with melted butter. Crease and fold over. Place on a greased baking sheet.

Cloverleaf Rolls: Break off pieces of dough and form into 3/4-inch balls. Place 3 balls in greased muffin cups. Brush lightly with melted butter before baking.

Cover loosely with plastic wrap that has been dusted with flour. Allow to rise until doubled. Preheat oven to 400 degrees. Bake rolls until golden, about 8-10 minutes.

Yields 4 dozen Parkerhouse rolls or 2 dozen Cloverleaf rolls

As these rich and golden rolls bake, the wonderful aroma that fills the air is the invitation to taste them as they emerge warm from the oven.

Oatmeal Molasses Bread

2½ cups boiling water
2 cups rolled old fashioned oats
1½ tablespoons salt
1/3 cup sulphured molasses
3 teaspoons salad oil
2 packages dry yeast
1/2 cup warm water
1/2 teaspoon sugar
6 cups flour

Mix the boiling water, oats, salt, molasses and oil. Allow to cool to lukewarm, about 25 minutes. Dissolve the yeast with the sugar in the warm water. Allow to become bubbly. Stir 3 cups of the flour into the cooled oat mixture. Blend well. Add the yeast mixture and the remaining flour. Mix well. Turn onto well floured surface and knead until smooth and no longer sticky. Place in a clean, dry bowl, covered, and allow to rise until doubled.

Punch down. Divide dough in half. Flatten into rectangles and roll in jelly roll fashion into loaves. Place seam side down in two greased 8½ x 4½-inch loaf pans. Cover with plastic wrap that has been dusted with flour. Allow to rise until doubled and above the edge of the pan.

Preheat oven to 350 degrees. Bake loaves until they are golden and sound hollow when tapped, approximately 40-45 minutes. Brush with melted butter and cool on rack after removing from pans.

Yields 2 loaves

Applesauce Nut Bread

1¼ cups unsweetened applesauce
1 cup sugar
1/2 cup oil
2 eggs
3 tablespoons milk
2 cups flour
1 teaspoon baking soda
1/2 teaspoon baking powder
1/2 teaspoon cinnamon
1/2 teaspoon salt
1/4 teaspoon nutmeg
1/4 teaspoon allspice
1/2 cup chopped pecans

Topping
1/4 cup chopped pecans
1/4 cup dark brown sugar
1/2 teaspoon cinnamon

Preheat oven to 350 degrees.

Combine applesauce, sugar, oil, eggs
and milk. Mix well. Sift together the
dry ingredients and spices. Stir into the
applesauce mixture. Fold in pecans.
Mix well. Spoon into two well buttered
8½ x 4½-inch loaf pans. Combine topping ingredients and sprinkle over the
2 loaves. Bake until bread pulls away
from sides of pans and tester comes out
clean when inserted in center, 50-60
minutes. Cool briefly in the pans, then
turn onto a rack.

Yields 2 loaves

Pineapple Pecan Bread

4 tablespoons butter, softened
3/4 cup sugar
2 eggs
1¾ cups flour
2 teaspoons baking powder
1/2 teaspoon salt
1/4 teaspoon baking soda
1/2 cup chopped pecans
1 cup crushed unsweetened pineapple,
    partially drained
1½ teaspoons cinnamon sugar

Preheat oven to 350 degrees.

Cream butter and sugar until fluffy.
Add the eggs, beating well. Combine
the dry ingredients. Add about 1/2 of
the dry ingredients with the nuts to
the creamed mixture. Stir well. Add the
pineapple and the rest of the flour mixture. Stir until blended. Spoon batter
into an 8½ x 4½-inch loaf pan that has
been greased and lined with wax paper
on the bottom. Sprinkle with cinnamon sugar. Bake until tester comes out
clean when inserted in center, approximately 45-50 minutes. Cool on rack.

Yields 1 loaf

Blue Ribbon Zucchini Bread

2 eggs
1 cup vegetable oil
2 cups grated unpeeled zucchini
2 cups sugar
1/4 teaspoon pepper
1 teaspoon salt
2 teaspoons baking soda
2 teaspoons cinnamon
2¼ cups flour
2 teaspoons vanilla
1 cup chopped walnuts

Preheat oven to 350 degrees.

Butter two 8½ x 4½-inch loaf pans.
Line bottoms of pans with wax paper
to avoid sticking. In a large bowl,
beat the eggs, then add the oil and zucchini. Add the remaining ingredients,
one at a time. Mix and beat well. Pour
into prepared pans. Bake until tester
comes out clean when inserted in center, about 1 hour. Cool briefly in pans,
then turn onto rack.

Yields 2 loaves

Sherry Currant Scones

3/4 cup currants
1/3 cup dry sherry
2 cups flour
2½ teaspoons baking powder
1 teaspoon salt
1½ tablespoons sugar
6 tablespoons butter
1/2 cup milk
2 egg yolks, beaten
1 egg white, beaten with 1 tablespoon
   water
Sugar

Preheat oven to 425 degrees.

Soak the currants in the sherry.
Measure the dry ingredients into a large
bowl. Cut in the butter until crumbly.
Combine the milk and egg yolks. Add
drained plumped currants to the milk
mixture. Gently mix with dry
ingredients until a soft dough is
formed.

On a floured surface, roll into a circle
about 1/2-inch thick. Place on a lightly
greased baking sheet. Score into pie
shaped wedges. Brush lightly with egg
white glaze. Sprinkle with sugar. Bake
until light brown, approximately 12-15
minutes.

Yields 1 dozen scones

*These scones, studded with sherry mari-
nated currants, are the perfect accompaniment to a cup of English Tea.*

Finnish Braided Bread

2 packages dry yeast
1/4 cup warm water
1/2 cup butter
3/4 cup milk
1/2 cup sugar
1 egg, beaten
1/2 teaspoon salt
1½ teaspoons ground cardamom
3½ to 4 cups flour
Egg glaze (1 egg beaten with 1
   tablespoon water)
Sugar

Dissolve yeast in warm water and allow
to become bubbly. Melt butter in a small
saucepan. Add milk and sugar. Cool to
lukewarm. Mix yeast, butter mixture,
egg, salt, and cardamom with half of
the flour until smooth. Gradually, add
the remaining flour. Knead until dough
is smooth but soft. Place in a clean bowl.
Let rise until doubled, about 1 hour.

Punch down dough. Knead briefly,
adding extra flour if necessary. Divide
dough in half. Divide each half into
3 equal parts. Roll each section into
long ropes and braid ropes together,
tucking ends under. Place braids diagonally on a well greased 12 x 18-inch
baking sheet. Brush lightly with egg
glaze. Cover with plastic wrap that has
been dusted with flour. Allow to
double in size, about 45 minutes.

Preheat oven to 375 degrees. Again,
brush braids gently with egg glaze.
Sprinkle with sugar. Bake until golden,
approximately 18-20 minutes.

Yields 2 loaves

Lemon Glazed Muffins

3/4 cup sugar
2 large eggs, beaten
1 cup plain yogurt
4 tablespoons butter, melted
1 tablespoon grated lemon zest
1/2 cup finely chopped walnuts
2 cups flour
1 teaspoon baking powder
1 teaspoon baking soda
1/2 teaspoon salt

Topping
1/3 cup fresh lemon juice
1/3 cup sugar
1½ tablespoons water

Preheat oven to 375 degrees.

In a large bowl, combine the sugar, eggs,
yogurt, butter, zest and walnuts. Mix
well. Combine the dry ingredients and
add to the creamed mixture. Stir
briefly, only until combined. Spoon
into buttered muffin tins, filling about
3/4 full. Bake until golden and tester
comes out clean when inserted in center, 15-20 minutes.

While muffins are baking, combine
topping ingredients in a small saucepan and boil for 1 minute. After removing muffins from oven, cool for 5
minutes in tin. Gently, pierce top of
the muffins several times with a fork.
Spoon 2 teaspoons of the cooked syrup
over the top of each muffin. Cool
briefly in the pan, then turn out onto
a rack.

Yields 10 muffins

Hazelnut Muffins

4 tablespoons butter
1/4 cup light brown sugar
1/3 cup sugar
1 egg
1 cup sour cream
1¾ cups flour
2 teaspoons baking powder
1 teaspoon baking soda
1/2 teaspoon salt
1/4 teaspoon allspice
1/2 cup chopped hazelnuts, with skins

Topping
1 tablespoon butter, softened
2 tablespoons light brown sugar
2 tablespoons ground hazelnuts, with
    skins

Preheat oven to 400 degrees.

Cream the butter with the sugars. Add
the egg and beat until fluffy. Stir in the
sour cream. Combine all the dry
ingredients and chopped nuts. Add to
the creamed mixture, stirring only to
combine. Spoon into greased or lined
muffin tins, filling about 2/3 to 3/4 full.

Topping: Cream the softened butter
with the sugar and add the ground
nuts. Divide topping evenly over the
batter-filled muffin tins. Bake for
approximately 18 minutes, or until
golden brown and tester comes out
clean when inserted in center. Cool on
rack.

Yields 1 dozen muffins

Brown Bread Muffins

1 large egg
1/4 cup sulphured molasses
2/3 cup dark brown sugar
1/3 cup salad oil
1 cup buttermilk or soured milk
1/2 cup rye flour
1/2 cup cornmeal
1/2 cup whole wheat flour
1/2 teaspoon salt
1½ teaspoons baking soda
1/2 cup raisins or currants, coated with
    1 teaspoon flour

Preheat oven to 400 degrees.

In a large bowl, combine the egg,
molasses, sugar, oil and milk. Mix well.
Add the dry ingredients and stir briefly
to combine. Gently stir in the raisins,
only to combine with batter. Spoon
into greased or lined muffin tins, filling
about 2/3 to 3/4 full. Bake for 15-18
minutes or until tester comes out clean.
Cool on rack. Serve with cream cheese.

Yields 18 muffins

*Akin to the steamed brown bread of New
England, these muffins serve as wonderful breakfast fare or as a complement to
soups or salad.*

Sunshine Muffins

2 oranges
3 tablespoons butter, softened
3/4 cup sugar
1 large egg, beaten
1¾ cups flour
1 teaspoon baking powder
1 teaspoon baking soda
1/2 teaspoon salt
2 teaspoons grated orange zest

Preheat oven to 400 degrees.

Remove pulp and juice from 2 oranges
to measure 1/2 cup. Set aside.

Cream the butter and sugar. Add the
egg and beat until fluffy. Combine the
dry ingredients and orange zest. Add
to the creamed mixture and stir gently.
Add the orange pulp and juice. Mix
only to combine. Spoon into greased or
lined muffin tins. Fill 3/4 full. Bake for
15-18 minutes, until golden and tester
comes out clean when inserted in center. Cool on rack.

Yields 10 muffins

Desserts

Chocolate Ganache

Chocolate Ganache
9 ounces semi-sweet baking chocolate
5 egg yolks
1/2 cup sugar
2 ounces Tia Maria
1 teaspoon vanilla
1 cup unsalted butter, softened
1⅓ cups cocoa powder
2 cups heavy cream
1/4 cup confectioners sugar, sifted
1 teaspoon vanilla

Pistachio Crème Anglaise
4 egg yolks
1 teaspoon vanilla
1/4 cup sugar
2 cups heavy cream
1/4 cup chopped pistachios

Strawberry Purée
1½ cups fresh strawberries
3 tablespoons sugar

Chocolate Ganache: Melt chocolate in double boiler. Whisk egg yolks and sugar together until light and lemon colored. Whisk in Tia Maria, 1 teaspoon vanilla and melted chocolate.

In large bowl of mixer, sift cocoa powder over softened butter. Beat on low speed until combined. Increase speed and beat until well creamed. Add chocolate mixture and beat until blended.

Beat 2 cups of heavy cream until soft peaks form. Gradually add confectioners sugar and 1 teaspoon vanilla, continuing to beat until stiff peaks form. Stir 1 cup into chocolate mixture to lighten. Fold in remaining whipped cream. Pour into a 10-inch ring mold and refrigerate.

Pistachio Crème Anglaise: Place egg yolks, vanilla and sugar in a double boiler. Cook over hot water, whipping constantly until doubled in volume and slightly thickened. Chill. When completely chilled, add heavy cream and all but 1 tablespoon of the pistachios (to be used for garnish). Mix thoroughly and refrigerate.

Strawberry Purée: Place strawberries and sugar in food processor or blender; purée until smooth.

To Assemble: Dip mold in warm water to loosen. Turn out onto a serving platter. Fill center of ring with fresh fruits such as strawberries, pineapple, kiwi and melon. Serve the crème anglaise and strawberry purée in separate pitchers on the side. If served individually, spoon crème anglaise onto cold plate and swirl to cover uniformly. Spoon a small amount of strawberry purée onto the plate and with a knife create a design, swirling the purée into the anglaise. Place ganache on top of the sauce. Garnish with fresh fruit and a sprinkling of pistachios.

Serves 16-18

Lady 'n Amaretto

3-4 packages ladyfingers
Amaretto to taste

4 8-ounce packages cream cheese, softened
2 eggs
1 cup sugar
1/3 cup Amaretto
2½ cups sliced strawberries

2 cups heavy cream
1 teaspoon vanilla
3 tablespoons confectioners sugar
10 whole strawberries
1/4 cup toasted almonds

Layer bottom of trifle bowl with split ladyfingers; sprinkle lightly with Amaretto.

Cream softened cream cheese with eggs, sugar and 1/3 cup Amaretto until smooth. Spread half of cream cheese mixture over ladyfingers. Top with half of the sliced strawberries. Add another layer of ladyfingers; sprinkle with Amaretto. Spread rest of cream cheese mixture over ladyfingers. Top with rest of strawberries. Top with ladyfingers.

Whip cream with vanilla and confectioners sugar; place in pastry bag and decorate top of torte. Garnish with whole strawberries and almonds.

Serves 12

Espresso Cheesecake

Crust
1 cup semi-sweet chocolate chips
1¼ cups vanilla wafer crumbs
2½ tablespoons sugar
6 tablespoons butter, melted and
    cooled

Filling
2 tablespoons ground espresso coffee
2/3 cup boiling water
3 8-ounce packages cream cheese,
    softened
1 cup sugar
2 eggs
1 cup dairy sour cream
1 8-ounce package semi-sweet
    chocolate squares, melted
1 teaspoon vanilla extract

1 cup heavy cream
Sugar
Chocolate-covered espresso beans,
    available in gourmet shops

Preheat oven to 350 degrees.

Crust: Place chocolate chips in blender
or food processor; process until slightly crushed. Mix with wafer crumbs,
sugar and melted butter. Press into the
bottom and up sides of a 9-inch springform pan.

Make a strong extract of espresso with
ground espresso and boiling water.
Brew in any coffee maker or pour boiling water over grounds placed in cheesecloth lined strainer over a bowl. Measure 1/2 cup and cool.

Filling: In a large mixer bowl, beat
cream cheese, sugar and eggs until
blended. Beat in sour cream, chocolate,
espresso concentrate and vanilla. Pour
into crumb-lined pan. Bake for 45
minutes or until puffed at sides. Cool,
then chill 3 hours or more, until center
is firm.

Whip remaining 1 cup cream with
sugar to taste.

Loosen crust on all sides using sharp
knife. Remove springform sides. To
serve, cut into wedges and garnish with
a dollop of whipped cream and a
chocolate-covered espresso bean.

Serves 12

*A heavenly chocolate dessert that satisfies
the after-dinner desire for coffee and
sweets.*

Pavlova

4 jumbo egg whites
1 cup superfine sugar
2 tablespoons boiling water
1 teaspoon vanilla
1 teaspoon malt vinegar
2 tablespoons superfine sugar
Whipped cream, sweetened to taste
Strawberries, blueberries, kiwi or other
    seasonal fruits

Preheat oven to 350 degrees. Line
baking sheet with lightly greased and
floured foil. Draw an 8-inch circle on
the floured surface.

Beat egg whites with sugar, boiling
water, vanilla and malt vinegar until
sugar is dissolved and stiff peaks form.
Add 2 extra tablespoons of sugar, one
at a time, and beat again until stiff
and sugar is dissolved, approximately
6-10 minutes. Spread meringue evenly
over circle, either with a spatula or
through a pastry bag. Bake for 10 minutes; reduce heat to 250 degrees and
bake for 10 more minutes; reduce heat
to 150 degrees and bake for 1¼ hours.
Turn oven off and allow pavlova to
cool in oven with door slightly open.

To serve, carefully peel away foil. Place
pavlova on serving dish and cover with
whipped cream and fruit of your
choice.

Serves 8

White Velvet Tart

Crust
2 cups chocolate wafer crumbs
1/3 cup unsalted butter, melted

Filling
1 cup fresh raspberries
1 tablespoon granulated sugar
1 teaspoon cornstarch
6 ounces white chocolate, finely
  chopped
3/4 cup unsalted butter, room
  temperature
8 tablespoons superfine sugar
3 eggs

Decoration
2 ounces semi-sweet chocolate
1 teaspoon unsalted butter
1 teaspoon vegetable oil

Crust: Combine crumbs and butter. Press onto bottom of 10-inch springform pan. Chill.

Filling: Purée the raspberries; bring to a boil over medium heat with sugar and cornstarch. Cook until thickened. Cool slightly and spread over crumb crust. Set aside.

Soften chocolate in top of double boiler over simmering water. In a separate bowl, cream butter; gradually add sugar, one tablespoon at a time, until pale yellow. Stir in the warm chocolate. Add eggs one at a time, beating for 3 minutes after each addition. Pour the filling into the crumb crust.

Decoration: In a small saucepan, melt chocolate and butter over very low heat. Add the oil and mix well. Cool slightly. Using a pastry bag fitted with a small plain tip, pipe a spiral circle of chocolate on top of tart. Chill for 7-10 minutes. Working with a sharp knife, start from the center of the tart and draw the knife outward to the edge of the tart pan, creating a spiral effect. Serve with fresh raspberries.

Serves 12

A crunchy dark chocolate crust topped with a thin layer of raspberry purée and filled with a satiny white chocolate mousse is a lovely way to finish a meal.

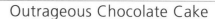

Outrageous Chocolate Cake

Cake
8 ounces semi-sweet chocolate
1 cup butter, room temperature
1 1/2 cups sugar
5 eggs, beaten

Ganache
12 ounces semi-sweet chocolate chips
1 cup heavy cream

1/2 pint raspberries

Preheat oven to 350 degrees.

Cake: In a double boiler, melt chocolate. Cool slightly. Add butter one tablespoon at a time, stirring after each addition. Add sugar and beat one minute. Add eggs and beat well. Pour batter into buttered 8-inch round cake pan lined with buttered waxed paper. Place the cake pan in a larger pan and pour boiling water into the larger pan to 1/2 way up the sides of the cake pan. Bake for 1 1/4 hours. Cool. Refrigerate 2 hours. Invert and spread with ganache.

Ganache: Briefly boil cream and chocolate. Refrigerate.

To Assemble: Invert cake onto serving platter. Spread with ganache. Refrigerate. To serve, cover top with berries.

Serves 14-16

Chocolate Mousse Pie

Crust
3 cups crushed chocolate wafer cookie
   crumbs
1/2 cup butter, melted

Filling
12 ounces semi-sweet chocolate chips
2 eggs
4 egg yolks
2 cups heavy cream
6 tablespoons confectioners sugar
4 egg whites, room temperature

Topping
2 cups heavy cream
Sugar to taste

Chocolate Leaves
6 ounces semi-sweet chocolate
1 tablespoon solid vegetable shortening
Waxy leaves

Crust: Combine cookie crumbs with butter. Press firmly onto bottom and up sides of a 10-inch springform pan. Chill for 30 minutes.

Filling: Melt chocolate in double-boiler, cool. Add whole eggs and mix well. Add yolks; mix well. In small mixer bowl, whip cream with confectioners sugar. In a separate bowl, beat egg whites until stiff. Stir a small amount of whipped cream and egg whites into chocolate mixture. Fold in remaining whipped cream and egg whites. Pour into crust and chill overnight.

Topping: Whip cream with sugar until stiff. Spread on mousse. Refrigerate. When ready to serve, loosen crust with a knife and remove from springform pan.

Chocolate Leaves: In a small saucepan, melt chocolate and shortening over low heat. Spoon melted chocolate onto the underside of leaves. Chill until firm. Carefully peel chocolate from leaves. Arrange on top of mousse.

Serves 12

A crunchy chocolate crust envelopes a rich creamy chocolate mousse. A perfect dessert for company because it can be made a day ahead and garnished just before serving.

Almond Charlotte

24 ladyfingers
6 tablespoons butter, softened
4 egg yolks
1 cup sugar
1⅔ cups ground almonds
1¼ teaspoons almond extract
1 cup heavy cream

1 cup heavy cream
1 tablespoon sugar
Whole blanched almonds

Line both sides and bottom of a 7-inch charlotte pan or springform pan with parchment paper. Place ladyfingers around inside of pan and across bottom. Those placed around the sides should stand on their ends with the flat side facing inside the pan.

In a large mixer bowl, combine softened butter, egg yolks, sugar, ground almonds, almond extract and heavy cream. Beat well. Pour 1/2 of mixture into pan. Place one layer of ladyfingers on top and cover with remaining mixture. Place a layer of ladyfingers on top. Crush excess ladyfingers to fill in all crevices. Cover top with cheesecloth and weigh down with pie weights. Refrigerate overnight.

When ready to serve, unmold onto serving platter. Whip cream and sugar until stiff. Spread half of whipped cream over top. Using a pastry bag fitted with a rosette tip, pipe remaining whipped cream onto top to decorate. Garnish with almonds.

Serves 6-8

Italian Cream Cake

Cake
1/2 cup butter
1/2 cup oil
2 cups sugar
5 eggs, separated
1 teaspoon baking soda
2 cups flour, sifted
1 cup buttermilk
1½ teaspoons vanilla
1¼ cups grated coconut
1/2 cup pecans, chopped

Icing
1 8-ounce package cream cheese, softened
1/2 cup butter, softened
1 teaspoon vanilla
1 pound confectioners sugar, sifted
1/2 cup pecans, chopped, roasted

Preheat oven to 325 degrees. Grease and lightly flour 3 9-inch cake pans.

Cake: In a large mixer bowl, combine butter, oil and sugar; beat until creamy. Add the egg yolks, one at a time, beating after each addition. Stir baking soda into flour. Add flour mixture alternately with buttermilk. Add vanilla, coconut and nuts.

In a separate bowl, beat egg whites until stiff peaks form. Fold into cream mixture. Pour into prepared cake pans. Bake for 45 minutes. Cool.

Icing: Beat together cream cheese and butter. Add vanilla, confectioners sugar and pecans.

To Assemble: Place one cake layer, bottom side up, on a serving platter. Cover with a layer of icing. Top with a second cake layer, bottom side up, and cover with a layer of icing. Top with remaining cake layer, rounded side up, and frost top and sides with remaining icing.

Serves 10-12

Tall and gorgeous, this moist cake is filled with coconut and pecans and layered with a rich cream cheese icing ... a simply luscious creation.

Amaretto-Amaretti Fudge Pie

Crust
1 ounce unsweetened chocolate
6 tablespoons unsalted butter
1¼ cups crushed imported amaretti biscuits
1/2 cup chocolate wafer crumbs

Filling
3 ounces unsweetened chocolate
8 tablespoons unsalted butter
4 large eggs, room temperature
1/4 teaspoon salt
1½ cups sugar
3 tablespoons light corn syrup
1/4 cup heavy cream
1 teaspoon vanilla
2 tablespoons Amaretto

Whipped cream

Preheat oven to 350 degrees.

Crust: In top of double boiler, melt chocolate with butter and cool; mix with crushed amaretti biscuits and chocolate wafer crumbs. Spread in bottom and 1/3 up the sides of a 9-inch springform pan. Chill.

Filling: In top of double boiler, melt chocolate and butter; remove from heat and cool. In bowl of mixer beat together eggs and salt; gradually add sugar, beating until thick and pale. Beat in the corn syrup, heavy cream, vanilla, Amaretto and chocolate mixture. Pour into crust. Bake for 45 minutes. Cool. Serve with a dollop of whipped cream.

Serves 14-16

Celebration Torte

Meringues
6 large egg whites
Pinch salt
1/4 teaspoon cream of tartar
1¼ cups sugar

Chocolate Filling
8 ounces semi-sweet chocolate
4 tablespoons water
4 cups heavy cream
1/3 cup superfine sugar

1½ pints strawberries

Preheat oven to 225 degrees.

Meringues: Beat egg whites with salt and cream of tartar until stiff. Gradually add sugar, continuing to beat until meringue is like marshmallow. Line 2 baking sheets with lightly greased and floured foil. Draw 3 8-inch circles on the floured surface. Spread the meringue evenly over the circles, either with spatula or through a pastry bag. Bake l hour until meringues are pale gold but pliable. Remove from oven, peel foil and put on rack to dry.

Chocolate Filling: In a small saucepan, melt the chocolate and water over low heat. Cool; set aside. Whip the cream until it forms soft peaks. Slowly add superfine sugar and beat until very stiff; set aside.

To Assemble: Wash, dry and thinly slice strawberries, saving 6-8 uniform whole berries for top. Place one meringue layer on a serving plate and spread with a thin layer of chocolate. Spread on a layer of whipped cream and top with a layer of sliced berries. Put on second meringue and repeat procedure. Top with third layer and ice with chocolate. Spread whipped cream over top and sides carefully. Decorate top with whipped cream rosettes. Dip tops of whole berries in chocolate and place around cake. Refrigerate until ready to serve.

Serves 16-20

Truly a gift for a celebrated occasion. The steps to its perfection are simple if taken one by one.

Sweetheart Creams

1½ cups ripe raspberries
1 ripe banana, peeled and sliced
1/4 cup freshly squeezed lime juice
1/4 cup freshly squeezed orange juice
1 teaspoon lime zest
1 teaspoon orange zest
1½ cups sugar
4 cups milk
Fresh raspberries for garnish
Mint leaves for garnish

In medium bowl, crush together raspberries and bananas. Add fruit juices and blend into a coarse purée. Add fruit zests, sugar and milk and blend thoroughly. Pour mixture into an 8-cup heart-shaped mold or divide evenly among individual heart-shaped molds and freeze until firm.

To serve, dip mold(s) briefly in hot water to loosen edges. Turn out onto serving platter or plates and garnish with fresh raspberries and mint leaves.

Serves 8

Triple Buttercream Torte

Meringues
10 ounces blanched almonds, toasted
3/4 cup sugar
1/4 cup flour
8 egg whites, room temperature
1/3 teaspoon cream of tartar
1/3 teaspoon salt
1/4 cup sugar

Buttercream
1 1/2 cups sugar
1/3 cup plus 3 tablespoons water
12 egg yolks, room temperature
2 cups unsalted butter, room
    temperature

1 teaspoon vanilla
1 teaspoon instant coffee moistened
    with 1/4 teaspoon hot water
5 ounces semi-sweet chocolate, melted
    and cooled

Preheat oven to 350 degrees. Oil 3 9-inch cake pans and line bottoms with oiled waxed paper. Dust with flour. Reduce oven to 300 degrees.

Meringues: In food processor, finely grind toasted almonds. Add sugar and flour; blend well. In a large bowl, beat egg whites until foamy. Add cream of tartar and salt and continue to beat until soft peaks form. Slowly add sugar and beat until stiff but not dry. Gently fold in nut mixture, 2 tablespoons at a time. Spread batter evenly into cake pans and bake for 45 minutes. Remove from oven and cool slightly. Gently remove from pans and cool completely.

Buttercream: Combine sugar and water in small heavy saucepan. Cover and bring to boil over high heat. Reduce heat to medium and continue boiling, covered, 1 to 2 minutes. Remove cover and boil to soft ball stage (240 degrees). In large mixer bowl, beat egg yolks lightly on low speed. Increase speed to medium high and slowly pour syrup directly into yolks. Increase speed to high and continue beating until completely cooled. Reduce speed to medium and add butter, 1 tablespoon at a time, beating well after each addition. Increase speed to high and continue beating until creamy and thoroughly blended. Remove 1 1/2 cups buttercream and stir in vanilla; set aside. Remove 1 1/2 cups buttercream and stir in coffee concentrate; set aside. Stir cooled chocolate into remaining buttercream; set aside.

To Assemble: Place one meringue layer on a serving platter. Cover with coffee buttercream. Place second meringue on top and cover with vanilla buttercream. Place third meringue on top and cover sides and top with all but 1 cup of the chocolate buttercream. Place remaining buttercream in a pastry bag fitted with a rosette tip. Decorate top and sides of cake. Cool cake to set buttercream. Warm to room temperature to serve.

Serves 10-12

Coffee Tortoni and

Chocolate Sauce

Tortoni
1 egg white
Dash of salt
1 1/2 tablespoons sugar
1 tablespoon instant coffee
1 cup heavy cream
2 tablespoons sugar
1 teaspoon vanilla

Chocolate Sauce
12 ounces semi-sweet chocolate
7 ounces evaporated milk

1/4 cup toasted almonds

Tortoni: Combine egg white and dash of salt; beat until stiff. Add 1 1/2 tablespoons sugar and coffee and beat until shiny. In a separate bowl, beat cream, sugar and vanilla until stiff. Blend into coffee mixture and pour into a serving dish. Freeze. When ready to serve, remove from freezer and serve with hot Chocolate Sauce and sprinkle with toasted almonds.

Chocolate Sauce: Combine chocolate and milk in a double-boiler over hot water. Cook until satiny. Remove from heat and serve warm over tortoni. Can be refrigerated or frozen until ready to use.

Serves 4-6

Kahlua Torte

Chocolate Crust
1½ cups chocolate cookie crumbs
3 tablespoons melted butter

Kahlua Filling
4 teaspoons instant espresso
1 tablespoon hot water
4 eggs
1/2 cup sugar
1 cup heavy cream
3 tablespoons Kahlua

Garnish
Chocolate cookie crumbs
1 cup heavy cream, whipped
Grated chocolate

Crust: Mix together the chocolate cookie crumbs and melted butter. Press into the bottom of a 8-inch or 9-inch springform pan. Chill.

Filling: Dissolve the espresso in water; set aside. In a large mixer bowl, beat the eggs until light; continue beating while gradually adding sugar. Set the bowl over hot water and whisk until the mixture is warm to the touch. Return the bowl to the mixer and continue beating until the mixture has cooled. Beat in the coffee mixture. In a separate bowl, beat the heavy cream until soft peaks form. Add the Kahlua and beat until stiff. Fold into the egg mixture. Pour into the cookie-lined pan and freeze.

To serve: Remove sides of the pan. Press the chocolate cookie crumbs onto the sides of the torte. Using a pastry bag and a decorator tip, pipe whipped cream around the top of the torte. Sprinkle with grated chocolate.

Serves 10

Elegance with ease ... a creamy, refreshing Kahlua filling on a layer of chocolate cookie crumbs and topped with rosettes of sweetened whipped cream.

Crème Brûlée

4 cups heavy cream
1/4 cup plus 2 teaspoons sugar
8 egg yolks
2 teaspoons vanilla
1 cup light brown sugar

Preheat oven to 325 degrees.

Heat cream in a heavy saucepan over low heat just to boiling point. Add sugar and stir to dissolve. In a large bowl, beat yolks briefly with whisk. Pour hot cream in a slow, steady stream into the yolks, whisking constantly. Whisk in vanilla. Pour custard into a 6-cup custard dish, or a shallow baking dish. The custard should come to within 1 inch of the top of the dish. Place the custard dish in a larger pan and pour boiling water into the larger pan halfway up the sides of the dish. Bake for 30 minutes or until a sharp knife inserted in the center comes out clean. Remove from hot water bath and place on cooling rack. Cool to room temperature. Refrigerate 6-8 hours or overnight.

To serve: Sprinkle the brown sugar through a strainer until the custard is covered evenly and lightly. Place custard dish in a larger container filled with ice. Place all under broiler until lightly browned all over, about 3-4 minutes. Be careful not to allow the sugar to burn. Remove from heat. Cool until sugar hardens. Crack sugar topping and spoon into individual dishes.

Serves 8

Italian Pumpkin Pie

Crusts
2 cups graham cracker crumbs
1/2 cup sugar
1/2 teaspoon ginger
1/2 teaspoon cinnamon
1/2 cup butter, melted

Pumpkin Filling
6 eggs, separated
1½ pounds cream cheese
1⅓ cups sugar
1/4 teaspoon salt
2 cups canned pumpkin
3 tablespoons molasses
3 tablespoons Amaretto
2 teaspoons ginger
2 teaspoons cinnamon
1 cup heavy cream

Topping
1 cup heavy cream
Amaretto to taste

Preheat oven to 350 degrees.

Crusts: Combine cracker crumbs, sugar, ginger, cinnamon and melted butter. Line 2 9-inch pie pans, pressing firmly.

Filling: Beat egg whites until stiff peaks form; set aside. Combine all other ingredients and blend until smooth. Fold into the beaten egg whites. Pour into the two shells, dividing evenly. Bake until set in center, approximately 25 minutes.

When ready to serve, whip cream until stiff peaks form. Add Amaretto to taste. Slice the pie and serve each piece with a dollop of the flavored whipped cream.

Serves 16

Do not wait for a holiday to prepare this marvelous dessert. Elegant and luscious, it will delight year-round.

Simply Pecan Pie

9-inch unbaked pie shell

1/2 cup butter
1 cup light corn syrup
1 cup sugar
3 eggs, beaten
1/4 teaspoon lemon juice
1 teaspoon vanilla
Dash of salt
1 cup chopped pecans

Preheat oven to 425 degrees.

Brown butter in a saucepan until it is golden brown. Do not burn. Let cool.

In a separate bowl, combine ingredients in order listed. Blend in browned butter. Pour into unbaked pie shell and bake for 10 minutes, then lower oven temperature to 325 degrees and bake for an additional 40 minutes.

Serve warm with vanilla ice cream or whipped cream.

Serves 8

Sour Cream Streusel Apple Pie

Crust
1¾ cups flour
1/4 cup sugar
1 teaspoon cinnamon
1/2 teaspoon salt
3/4 cup butter
1/4 cup cold water

Filling
10 MacIntosh apples
1⅔ cups sour cream
1 cup sugar
1/3 cup flour
1 large egg, beaten
2 teaspoons vanilla
1/2 teaspoon salt

Topping
1/2 cup chopped walnuts
1/4 cup flour
3 tablespoons firmly packed brown sugar
3 tablespoons sugar
1/2 tablespoon cinnamon
Pinch of salt
1/4 cup butter

Preheat oven to 450 degrees.

Crust: In medium mixer bowl, combine flour, sugar, cinnamon and salt. Cut in butter until mixture resembles coarse meal. Gradually add water, tossing gently with fork. Form dough into a ball, then divide into 2 sections. Roll dough into two crusts.

Filling: Peel apples, then cut into thin slices. In large mixer bowl, combine apple slices, sour cream, sugar, flour, egg, vanilla and salt. Place one crust in a deep dish pie plate, pour in filling and cover with second crust. Flute edges, pierce crust several times. Bake for 10 minutes. Reduce heat to 350 degrees and continue baking for 40 minutes.

Topping: Combine all topping ingredients except butter; cut in butter until mixture resembles coarse meal. Spoon mixture on top of pie. Bake 15 minutes longer at 350 degrees.

Serves 6-8

A streusel is a crumbly topping made with flour, butter, sugar and cinnamon. This delicious sour cream apple pie is unique because it has a streusel topping which is added after the pie has baked and returned to the oven to brown.

Lime Tart

Crust
1¼ cups flour
1/3 cup confectioners sugar
1/3 teaspoon salt
5 ounces cold unsalted butter
1/2 cup chopped pecans

Lime Filling
5 tablespoons fresh lime juice
2 large eggs
1 cup sugar
1 teaspoon grated lime peel
1/2 teaspoon baking powder
1/2 teaspoon salt

Preheat oven to 350 degrees.

Crust: Combine flour, sugar and salt in bowl; cut in butter until mixture resembles coarse meal. Add chopped nuts to mixture and press into a 9-inch tart pan with removable bottom. Bake until golden brown, about 20 minutes. Remove shell from oven and let cool slightly.

Filling: Beat together lime juice and eggs; add sugar and lime peel and beat until smooth. Blend in baking powder and salt. Pour filling into shell. Be careful not to get filling behind crust. Bake an additional 25 minutes. Remove sides and bottom of tart pan and let tart cool completely on cooling rack. Sprinkle with confectioners sugar.

Serves 6

Grand Marnier Soufflé

Soufflé
2 egg whites
1 pinch salt
6 teaspoons sugar
1 cup heavy cream
1/3 cup sugar
1/4 cup Grand Marnier

Berry Sauce
1 pint fresh strawberries
1 pint fresh raspberries
Sugar to taste
Grand Marnier to taste

Fresh berries for garnish

Beat egg whites with pinch of salt until soft. Beat in 6 teaspoons of sugar very gradually until stiff peaks form; set aside.

In a large chilled mixer bowl, beat cream until soft peaks form. Gradually add 1/3 cup sugar and continue beating until stiff peaks form. Add Grand Marnier and mix gently with rubber spatula. Fold egg whites into cream mixture. Turn into a 1-quart ring mold or small freezer mold. Freeze until firm, at least 4 hours.

Sauce: Purée berries until smooth. Add sugar and Grand Marnier to taste.

To serve, unmold frozen soufflé onto a glass plate or silver tray. Garnish generously with fresh berries. Serve Berry Sauce on the side.

Hint: This recipe can be doubled or tripled. The soufflé can be made in advance and frozen and the sauce can be prepared ahead and kept in the refrigerator.

Serves 4

The delicate and creamy yellow soufflé contrasts beautifully with the tart and blushing red berry sauce ... a perfect choice for a company dessert.

Apricot Cheese Pillows

8 prepared crêpes
1 8-ounce package cream cheese, softened
1/4 cup butter, softened
1/4 cup sugar
1½ teaspoons vanilla
1 teaspoon grated lemon peel
2 tablespoons butter
1/2 cup toasted sliced almonds for garnish

Apricot Sauce
2/3 cup apricot preserves
1/3 cup orange juice
2 tablespoons butter
1 tablespoon lemon juice
1½ teaspoons grated lemon peel

Preheat oven to 350 degrees.

Pillows: In a small bowl of electric mixer, beat cream cheese, butter, sugar, vanilla and lemon peel until fluffy. Divide the mixture evenly among the crêpes and spread it almost to the edges of each. Fold each crêpe into thirds and then turn edges under forming a square. Arrange crêpes in a lightly buttered baking dish and dot with butter. Bake for 10 minutes in preheated oven. Remove crêpes and top with Apricot Sauce and toasted almonds.

Apricot Sauce: Combine preserves, orange juice, butter, lemon juice and lemon peel in a small saucepan; cook over low heat until smooth. Serve over warm crêpes.

Serves 8

Praline Ice Cream Cake

Cookies
1 cup flour
1/2 teaspoon salt
1/2 teaspoon baking soda
1/2 cup unsalted butter, room
    temperature
1/2 cup firmly packed light brown sugar
1/4 cup sugar
1 egg
1/2 teaspoon vanilla
1 cup pecans, coarsely chopped

2 pints butter pecan ice cream

1 cup heavy cream
1 tablespoon sugar

Caramel Sauce
1¼ cups sugar
3/4 cup water
1 cup cream

Preheat oven to 350 degrees.

Cookies: Sift together flour, salt and baking soda; set aside. Cream butter and sugars until smooth. Beat in egg and vanilla. Stir in flour mixture, then nuts. Drop dough onto lightly greased baking sheets, using 1½ teaspoons for each cookie and spacing 2 inches apart. Flatten with back of a fork dipped in water. Bake until cookies are light brown, about 7 minutes. Cool.

To Assemble: Oil an 8 x 4-inch loaf pan lined with aluminum foil. Completely cover pan bottom with a layer of cookies, flat sides down. Press half of ice cream firmly over cookies. Crumble 4 cookies and sprinkle over top. Press remaining ice cream firmly on top. Top with layer of 8 cookies, flat sides up. Cover and freeze at least one day.

Just before serving, invert onto platter. Refrigerate while preparing cream. Whip cream with 1 tablespoon sugar until stiff peaks form. Smooth 3/4 of the cream over sides of cake. Using a pastry bag, pipe rosettes over top of cake. Decorate with pecans. Freeze 5 minutes. Serve with warm Caramel Sauce.

Caramel Sauce: Heat sugar and water in a small heavy saucepan over low heat until sugar dissolves. Increase the heat to medium and boil, without stirring, until light brown. Meanwhile, bring cream to simmer in small heavy saucepan. Reduce heat to low and keep warm. Reduce heat under syrup to low and cook until golden brown. Gradually add warm cream. When the bubbling stops, mix well. If not served immediately, re-warm over very low heat.

Serves 8-10

How can anything so simple to prepare be so magnificent to serve? This is the beauty of this dramatic dessert.

Vanilla Pears in Galliano Sabayon

Poached Pears
3 cups water
1½ tablespoons fresh lemon juice
6 large pears, firm but ripe
2 cups water
1½ cups sugar
1 cup dry white wine
2 vanilla beans

Sabayon
4 large egg yolks
3/4 cup Galliano
1/3 cup sugar
1 cup heavy cream
Candied violets for garnish

Poached Pears: Place 3 cups of water and lemon juice in a large bowl. Carefully peel pears, leaving the stems on, and drop immediately into lemon water. In a 3-quart saucepan, combine 2 cups water, sugar, wine and vanilla beans; bring to a boil over high heat to dissolve the sugar. Transfer pears to the poaching liquid. Reduce the heat to medium and poach pears until tender, about 25 minutes. Allow pears to cool in the poaching liquid. Carefully remove pears. Arrange on serving plates. Chill.

Sabayon: Combine egg yolks, Galliano and sugar in the top of a double boiler. Whisk to blend and place over simmering water. Whisk constantly until mixture thickens, about 20 minutes. Do not allow mixture to boil. Transfer to a bowl and cool. Whip cream and fold into cooled mixture. Serve with chilled pears. Decorate with candied violets.

Serves 6

Meringue Baskets

6 egg whites, room temperature
1/4 teaspoon salt
1/4 teaspoon cream of tartar
1½ cups superfine sugar
1 teaspoon vanilla

Preheat oven to 225 degrees. Line a baking sheet with lightly greased and floured foil.

In a medium mixer bowl, beat egg whites with salt and cream of tartar until frothy. Gradually add the sugar, 3 tablespoons at a time, beating well after each addition. Add the vanilla and continue beating until stiff but not dry.

To form the baskets, use a pastry bag or a large spoon. Spread meringue evenly into 3-inch circles. Using a pastry bag, pipe a border to a height of about 1½-inches all around the circle or, using a spoon, shape the baskets into round or oval mounds.

Bake approximately 1 hour or until firm and dry. When the meringues are done, turn off the heat and leave them in the oven for another 15 minutes. When the meringues are cool, fill with your favorite ice cream and top with Rum Chocolate Sauce.

Serves 18-24

These meringue baskets can be made ahead and frozen. Only your imagination can limit what might fill them. Consider fresh raspberries drizzled with Kir or perhaps chocolate mousse and fresh strawberries.

Rum Chocolate Sauce

1/2 cup unsalted butter
1 cup sugar
1/3 cup sifted unsweetened cocoa powder
2 tablespoons dark rum
1 cup heavy cream
1/8 teaspoon salt
1 teaspoon dry instant coffee
1 teaspoon vanilla

In a medium saucepan, melt butter over low heat. Add sugar, cocoa, rum, heavy cream and salt. Stir over moderate heat until mixture comes to a boil. Add the instant coffee and stir to dissolve. Reduce heat and let simmer five minutes. Remove from heat and stir in vanilla.

Serve warm over meringue baskets filled with vanilla ice cream.

Store any remaining sauce in refrigerator. It will keep for weeks.

Yields 2 cups

Peach Crisp and Cream

Peach Crisp
1 cup flour
1/2 cup sugar
1/2 cup packed light brown sugar
1/2 teaspoon cinnamon
1/4 teaspoon grated nutmeg
1/4 teaspoon salt
1/2 cup butter, cut into pieces
5-6 cups peeled and sliced fresh peaches
Juice and grated zest of 1/2 lemon
2 tablespoons maple syrup

Maple Cream Sauce
1½ cups heavy cream
5 tablespoons maple syrup
3 tablespoons light corn syrup

Preheat oven to 350 degrees.

Peach Crisp: Combine flour, sugars, cinnamon, nutmeg and salt in a medium bowl. Cut in butter with a fork until mixture resembles coarse meal. Spread peaches into a lightly buttered 9-inch square baking dish. Gently mix in lemon juice, zest and maple syrup. Top with crumb mixture. Cover tightly with foil and bake for about 15 minutes. Remove foil and bake for an additional 30 minutes, or until top is crisp and browned. Serve warm with Maple Cream Sauce.

Maple Cream Sauce: Combine cream and syrups in a small saucepan. Cook over moderate heat, stirring constantly until thickened, about 20 minutes. Remove from heat and chill.

Serves 6

Viennese Sandwich Cookies

Cookies
6 tablespoons whole blanched almonds
1¼ cups flour
1/2 cup butter
1/3 cup sugar
1/4 teaspoon salt
1/4 cup apricot preserves

Chocolate Glaze
1/2 cup semi-sweet chocolate chips
1 tablespoon butter
1 tablespoon milk
1½ teaspoons corn syrup

Preheat oven to 350 degrees.

Cookies: In covered blender or food processor, blend the almonds until finely ground. Into a large bowl measure flour, butter, sugar and salt; add ground almonds. With hands, knead until well blended. Between waxed paper, roll dough 1/8-inch thick. Cut with 2-inch round cookie cutter. Place on ungreased cookie sheet and bake 8 minutes. Remove to wire racks to cool.

Chocolate Glaze: In a double boiler over low heat, melt the chocolate and butter. Add the milk and corn syrup and stir until blended.

To Assemble: Spread preserves thinly on flat side of half the cookies. Top with remaining cookies. Dip filled cookies, edgewise, into warm chocolate glaze to cover half the cookie. Place on waxed paper to set. Refrigerate.

Yields 18 cookies

Swedish Creams

Cookies
1 cup butter, softened
1/3 cup heavy cream
2 cups flour, sifted
Granulated sugar

Cream
6 tablespoons butter, softened
1 cup plus 2 tablespoons sifted confectioners sugar
2 large egg yolks
1½ teaspoons vanilla

Preheat oven to 375 degrees.

Cookies: In a medium mixer bowl, combine butter, heavy cream and flour until well blended; chill. On lightly floured surface, roll dough to 1/8-inch thickness. Cut with floured donut hole cutter. Sprinkle with granulated sugar and place on ungreased baking sheet; prick with a fork and bake for 7-9 minutes. Check after 5 minutes to make sure the cookies do not brown. Remove from oven and cool on racks.

Cream: Cream butter and sugar. Beat in egg yolks and vanilla. Tint with choice of food coloring. Spread half of the cookies with the cream. Top with remaining cookies.

These cookies can be frozen and removed 15-20 minutes before serving.

Yields 4 dozen cookies

Orange Oatmeal Cookies

1 cup flour
1/2 teaspoon baking soda
1/2 teaspoon baking powder
1/2 teaspoon salt
1/2 cup butter
1/2 cup brown sugar
1/2 cup sugar
1 egg
1 tablespoon orange juice
1 teaspoon grated orange peel
1 cup oatmeal
1/2 cup golden raisins

Preheat oven to 350 degrees.

In a small bowl, combine flour, baking soda, baking powder and salt; set aside.

In a large mixer bowl, combine butter and sugars; beat until creamy. Beat in egg, orange juice and orange peel. Gradually add flour mixture. Stir in oatmeal and raisins. Drop by rounded measuring tablespoons onto greased baking sheets. Bake 10-12 minutes.

Yields 36 cookies

The texture of oatmeal, the zest of orange and the sweetness of golden raisins come together to make a cookie that is simply perfection.

German Shortbread Bars

2 cups butter, room temperature
1 cup sugar
1 egg yolk
5 cups flour

Preheat oven to 300 degrees.

Cream butter, sugar and egg yolk in mixer. Add flour by hand and knead well. Spread into a jelly roll pan using a rolling pin to spread evenly. Prick the entire top with a fork. Bake on middle rack of the oven for 1 hour. Remove from oven and cut immediately into bars.

Variation: Chocolate lovers can create these buttery cookies by reducing the flour to 4 cups and adding 1 cup of unsweetened cocoa powder and 1 tablespoon of vanilla.

Yields 3 dozen bars

Peanut Butter Affairs

1 1/2 cups sifted flour
1/2 cup sugar
1/2 teaspoon soda
1/4 teaspoon salt
1/2 cup shortening
1/2 cup creamy peanut butter
1/4 cup light corn syrup
1 tablespoon milk
1/3 cup peanut butter

Preheat oven to 350 degrees.

Sift together dry ingredients. Cut in shortening and peanut butter until mixture resembles coarse meal. Blend in syrup and milk. Shape into 2-inch roll and chill. Slice 1/8 to 1/4-inch thick. Place half the slices on a greased cookie sheet. Spread each with 1 1/2 teaspoons peanut butter. Cover with remaining slices and seal edges with a fork. Bake until golden brown around the edges, about 12 minutes.

Yields 18 cookies

Sugared Butter Cookies

1 pound butter, room temperature
1 cup sugar
4 cups flour
1 tablespoon vanilla
Sugar

Preheat oven to 350 degrees.

In a medium size bowl, beat butter with sugar until creamy. Add the flour and vanilla and blend thoroughly. Drop by small spoonfuls onto ungreased cookie sheet. Press gently with fork dipped in sugar, sprinkling any remaining sugar over cookie. Bake for 10-12 minutes. Do not overbake. Allow to cool slightly and remove to wire racks to cool completely.

Yields 4 dozen cookies

Index

Index

Acknowledgments

Book Development Committee
Nancy Adams
Dorothy Binswanger
Barbara Carnecchia
Margaret Hawley
Catherine Klingel
Patricia McGill
Karen Nakahara
Christine Seybold
Mary Vaira
Patricia Webster

Marketing Committee
Sandra Borror-Jury
Gina Foley
Helenanne Lasher
Maggie McGuire
Heather Murphy
Melissa Nichols
Julie Schmidt
Cindy Williams

Production Committee
Susan Colehower
Amy Muse Lang
Emilie Lapham
Susan Mulle
Patricia Porter
Teri Stahller
Elizabeth Tyson

Master Testers

Appetizers
Barbara Gasper
Patti Hejl
Susan Jablokov
Susan Jones
Susan Mulle
Anna Cooke Smith
Holly Tubiash
Elizabeth Tyson
Donna West

Salads
Kitty Brey
Betsy Claghorn
Ellie Johnston
Emilie Lapham
Debbie Mason
Joanne M. Miller
Aileen Roberts
Laurie Schobelock

Seafood
Jane Acton
Anne Aspinwall
Joy Brown
Tracy Gkonos
Jane Harrington

Poultry
Mary Allison

Laura Anderson
Judy Bartle
Anne Brockman
Anne Krout
Alice Smith
Barbara Stolp

Meats
Betsy Agnew
Nancy Groff
Julia Hoekstra
Candy Kottyan
May Lynn O'Hara

Vegetables
Cindy Archer
Susan Colehower
Diana Mather
Sally Millier
Leora Natan
Robin Ryan
Susan Walden
Mary Wetmore

Pasta/Brunch
Sharon McNamara
Elizabeth Ross
Margaret Welsh
Cindy Williams

Breads
Jane Baumgardner
Pat Carlton
Leslie Marshall
Janet Martin
Heather Murphy
Lisa Perry
Dora Rogers
Barbara Sartorius
Jane Wagner
Jody Widing

Soups/Desserts
Marsha Bruce
Meg Hawley
Trinka Hillman
Ann Hyland
Suzzanne Kastendike
Kim Schuh
Susan Siebert
Anne Sly
Alida Torrence

Photography Contributors
The Foundation for Architecture
The Academy of Music
The Free Library of Philadelphia
The Rodin Museum
Office of the City Representative
  of Philadelphia
Wilma Theatre
Academy of Natural Sciences
The Franklin Institute
Philadelphia Zoo

Longwood Gardens
The Japanese House and
  Garden
Morris Arboretum
Fairmount Park Commission
National Park Service
Visitors Bureau
Philadelphia Museum of Art
Peter Lapham

Philadelphia Site Photography by
Alix Coleman
Marc Daniels
Harvey A. Duze
Larry A. De Young
Bob Emmott
Addison Geary
Richard Nibble
Susan Robins
Teri Stahller
Vicki Valerio

Prop Contributors
Elizabeth Bacher
Kathryn S. Biddle
Dorothy Binswanger
Elizabeth N. Borton
Nicoll Cadwalader Brinley
Diana Castillo
Meg Henkels
Marianne Keating
Carol MacGregor
Mrs. Eugenia McGill
Patricia McGill
Joan McGinnis-Benasutti
Patricia Porter
Kim Schuh
Ellen Shah
Mrs. James M. Skinner, Jr.
Teri Stahller
Marlene Waldron
Christine Wick

Recipe Contributors
Christina Abendroth
Jane Acton
Nancy H. Adams
Peggy Adams
Carolyn R. Aller
Mary Heisler Allison
Kristen Heffner Alpert
Marjorie Jones Alvord
Mrs. W. Disston Anderson
Susan Lee Anderson
Barbara Kreuter Applegate
Cynthia Hill Archer
Susan W. Arnold
Mary Jo Ashenfelter
Anne Irvin Aspinwall
Maureen A. Augenstein
Kere Averett

Judy Emery Baer
Wendelyn C. Bailey
Heather S. Bailey
Margaret J. Barnhart
Judith Cox Bartle
Jane Crawford Baumgardner
Margaret Hicks Baumgardner
Christine Belson-Smart
Joan McGinnis Benasutti
Pamela V. Berg
Anne M. Berry
Lynn Susan Besancon
Barbara Best
Mrs. Ralph E. Biddle, Jr.
Dolores M. Binner
Dorothy F. Binswanger
Virginia J. Black
Camille Bondi
Sandra Borror-Jury
Lois J. Bortle
Beverly S. Borton
Nancy F. Bowden
Deborah Hamilton Brengle
Katharine B. Brey
Maryann Bushey Brink
Nicoll Cadwalader Brinley
Elizabeth Broughton
Charlotte Waterbury Brown
Clarissa W. Brown
Joy S. W. Brown
Audrey M. Bruce
Marsha Anne Bruce
Mary P. Burr
Olive Burris
Candice Calabro
Barbara Carlson Cameron
Patricia M. Carlton
Phyllis B. Carter
Baldo M. Carnecchia, Jr.
Barbara Wolf Carnecchia
Stephanie M. Carr
Diana Castillo
Carolyn Boring Catching
Melissa Champlin
Cathy Cheney
Cathy Ciarrochi
Elizabeth W. Claghorn
Mrs. Peter G. Clifford
Leslie Lynch Clinton
Kimberlea Close
Beth G. Clouser
Janice Manzi Cohen
Alex Saijen Wood Cole
Susan Brown Colehower
Deborah S. Colgan
Karla Conly
Rhonda St. M. Conner
Kia Cox
Paula T. Craig
Becky Crews
Mrs. James D. Crutchfield

Esta B. Cunningham
Dale D'Angelo
Clare Frances Deff
Mrs. Miller Detrick
Paige E. DiLorenzo
Gale Fentress Donoghue
Karen Scolari Drury
Linda Harrison Dutton
Bobbie Eckman
Mary Hallock Edwards
Mary H. Ehret
Anne T. Elder
Frances Elliott
Lisa Ann Elliott
Joan S. Emerson
Barbara Larmon Failing
Robert W. Failing, D.D.S.
Joan Faulk
Elizabeth Hamilton Ferrall
Debbie Ferry
Jaimie Spector Field
Mrs. Richard Fisher
Donna M. Fodi
Regina Geus Foley
Mrs. D. Jackson Freese
Shele French
Kathy Friedmann
Elizabeth Sears Gadsden
Barbara Gasper
Elizabeth W. Gamble
Susan F. Gibbons
Betsy Gilpin
Beth Glouser
Muriel Glouser
Lisey Bennett Good
Trish Gorman
E. Lawrie Graves
Florianne T. Greer
Nancy W. Greytok
Pamela F. Grimm
Alison N. Grisemer
Nancy Groff
Nancy K. Groves
Missy Gullquist
Maura Nevin Gustafson
Mrs. George Hacking
Brenda Lowrey Hacklander
Gretchen Dome Hagy
Bette S. Hamilton
Joanne M. Hanna
Janet Hawley Hannum
Mrs. E. P. Hannum
Jane B. Harrington
Sondra Harris
Susan J. Harris
Lisa M. Hatheway
Deborah L. Hawkins
Margaret D. Hawley
Barbara Harrison Heaton
Mary Anderson Hejl
Patti Elliott Hejl

Judy Helman
Kate C. Henry
Arturo R. Hervada
Helen Hervada
Maria Hervada-Page
Louise Lark Hill
Katharine A. Hillman
Mary S. Hinds
Nancy Herd Hirschfeld
Mary G. Hodge
Julia Hockstra
Elizabeth H. Holleran
Kevin Holleran
Priscilla Holleran
Mary Cloud Hollingshead
Mrs. Louis Hood
Saundra E. Hopkin
Jill Horn
Ann Hourigan
Louise H. Huber
Mrs. John Y. Huber, III
Carol M. Hughes
Ellen Huyett
Lolly Isayeff
Betts Saunders Jackson
Emily Long Jackson
Cynthia Lee Johnson
Mimi Johnson
Shelley A. Johnson
Eleanor T. Johnston
Mercer T. Jones
Susan J. Jones
Barbara James Jordan
Diana M. Jordan
Ann G. Kampf
Jean Heflin Kane
Mrs. George H. Kastendike, IV
Michelle Keating
Jill Keefer-Hugill
Gail Riggs Kelley
Jane M. Kelly
Maura Mullen Kempf
Stacy A. Kendra
Mary Kay Kennedy
Mrs. William I. Kent
Melissa Kerper
Catherine T. Klingel
Mary F. Knake
Jeanne Kohn
Joanne Paskins Kreuter
Sally Krogstad
Mrs. John E. Krout
Mrs. Robert D. Lang
Emilie Lapham
Helenanne R. Lasher
Dr. Lars G. Leksell
Mrs. E. Harvey Lenderman, Jr.
Mrs. Thomas C. Leonards, Jr.
Giovanna Lewis
Nelly K. Lincoln
Sandy Moshonas Lindberg

Elaine M. Lisle
Vicki Frazier Lockridge
Dr. Ellen Angres Loeb
Reda Smith Long
Linda S. Luckens
Betsy Lundquist
Louise Ann Lutz
Christine M. Lytton
Carol Elder MacGregor
Jill MacDonald
Cynthia MacLeod
Mary Mackowick-McCorry
JoAnn Marie Magnatta
Patricia Albano Manzi
Leslie S. Marshall
Lindsey F. Marshall
Sanna A. Marshall
Janet Martin
Deborah Campbell Mason
Mrs. F. Robert Masters, Jr.
Madeline Masterson
Marjorie Matash
Diana J. Mather
Donna Ellington Mateer
Logan Rehr Mateer
Joan Mateer
Mary Jo Mayberry
Marianne Rice McClatchy
Myra L. McCormick
Eugenia H. McGill
Patricia McGill
Margaret McGuire
Laure McIlroy
Ethelmae McSparren
Margaret W. Meigs
Lucinda S. Mezey
Catherine A. Milioti
Elizabeth S. Miller
Joanne Merriman Miller
Sally Pearson Millier
Barbara Mohr
Kristin Monroe
Helen S. Montgomery
Ellen Borie Moreland
Kay Baker Mower
Susan L. Mulle
Jean E. Murdock
Karen J. Murdock
Fay S. Murray
Marianne S. Murray
Pamela A. Murray
Kathryn Kress Myers
Sherry Lee Myers
Karen Reuter Nagel
Karen S. Nakahara
Leora D. Natan
Mrs. Jack D. Neilsen
Mrs. John D. Neilson
Dave Newton
Mary Nolan
Susanne Nolan

Kelly McKim Nole
Kim Norrett
Dorothy K. O'Donnell
May Lynn O'Hara
Cynthia Craig Olds
Judith P. Osgood
Anne Osterholm
Nickolas Panas
Mimi Park
Jane Wykle Parker
Jane Patette
Kristine Austin Paulat
Nana Pearson
Paula S. Pettyjohn
Mrs. John D. Pickens
Nancy Pickert
Barbara B. Pilling
Mary Anne Poatsy
Patricia W. Porter
Nancy Shumaker Post
Virginia Brooks Price
Elizabeth B. Pryor
Lee H. Radsch
Delores D. Ramsay
Margherita L. Ramsay
Tara Daly Ranson
Marcie Reber
Elsie J. Reed
Mary Patricia Reynolds
Susan Carver Rice
Dawn Richardson
Joan Heeney Riddle
Marnie Holt Rigby
Adelina Minardi Rock
Teresa Rodriguez
Dora L. Rogers
Betty Rooney
Elizabeth Charles Ross
Judy Ruse
Barbara K. Ryan
Robin C. Ryan
Lane Sadler
Barbara V. Sartorius
Mrs. David Savinar
Dave Sawutz
Kathleen Sawutz
Patricia Schaffer
Julie Verbiest Schmidt
Mrs. John F. Schoenfelder
Laurie Candler Schohelock
Melissa Schroll
L. Kim Schuh
Barbara Scorzetti
Arlene Allman Seeger
Adele C. Seybold
Christine G. Seybold
Valerie M. Seybold
Evelyn B. Seymour
Cannie C. Shafer
Barbara Ann Sharon
Betty C. Shaw

Judith A. W. Sherry
Stephanie Shore
Elizabeth Martin Shuman
Sandy Shute
Charles E. Skinner
Mrs. James M. Skinner, Jr.
Anne Alvord Sly
Christine B. Smart
Alice Gerow Smith
Alice Livingstone Smith
Anna Cooke Smith
Craig Corydon Smith
Carol Jackson Smith
Jeanette Smith
Roddy V. Smith
Peggy Hopper Sobota
Lynn Soisson
Morris Solotorovsky
Leslie M. Spilman
Karen McGuckin Spofford
Ellen V. A. Starratt
Lucy C. Statzell
Bill Stauffer
Gayle Stauffer
Lucie B. Steele
James B. Stern
Mrs. James B. Stern
Mary Jane Stitt
Kim Neuhoff Stokoe
Madeline L. Story
Fiona Strafford
Stacy W. Sullivan
Sally Y. Swanson
Leslie Burnett Swope
Nancy Swope
Chris Talone
Anita D. Taylor
Susan Tabas Tepper
Mrs. Michael B. Torrence
Petra Tratnik
Carl Tremaglio
Victoria M. Tremaglio
Diane Trout
Holly Elizabeth Tubiash
Sarah Preston Tubiash
Leigh E. Twiford
Peter F. Vaira, Jr.
Mary H. Vaira
Mrs. Peter F. Vaira, Sr.
Joyce Van Dyke
Elizabeth Van Fossen
H. Wade VanLandingham
Nancy Murdock VanLandingham
Marilyn Elder Van Ormer
Amy J. Van Schaick
Suzanne VanderVeer
Carol Verhake
Paula A. Verkuilen
Susan Kelly von Medicus
Jody Ann Wagner
Wendy Waite

Susan Walden
Jeanne Waldron
Mrs. Thomas A. Waldron
Kim Walker
Barbara Waller
Bonnie McBratney Wallin
Mary C. Walto
Eileen Wolfgram Ware
Patricia E. Webster
Cynthia Weierman
Anne Wetherill
Donna Marva West
Gigi Westbrook
Isabel E. Wheat
Virginia J. Whelan
Jody Widing
Susanne S. Widing
Cynthia Higgins Williams
Gail Dodge Williams
Mrs. Harding G. Williams
Scottie Williams
Terri Mayson Williams
Richard B. Wills
Jane Willson
Gayle Wilson-French
Melinda Waters Wohlstetter
Deborah L. Wolf
Mary Lou Ramsay Wolf
Mrs. William R. Wood
N. Virginia Woolridge
Elizabeth A. Wright
Karen S. Wymard
Joan Spece Yannessa
Karyn Hope Yost
Sally McKean Young
Victoria Loeb Ziss
Susan Zonino
Elizabeth Zug

The Cookbook Committee also wishes to express our gratitude to the supportive friends and family members whose names are not listed but whose efforts will be rewarded in the good works which Settings *will make possible.*